LAWS OF SUCCESS

12 LAWS THAT TURN DREAMS INTO REALITY

LES BROWN

Published & Distributed By:
Lurn, Inc.
Lurn Publishing Division
12410 Milestone Center Drive, Suite 600,
Germantown, MD 20876
www.lurn.com
ISBN-13: 978-0-9972079-3-4

TABLE OF CONTENTS

INTRODUCTION:
MRS. MAMIE BROWN'S BABY BOY

I often introduce myself as "Mamie Brown's Baby Boy." My mother, Mamie Brown was one of the most important people in my life. She instilled greatness in me. She never gave up on my brother Wesley or me. She showed me that no matter what the odds were, you had to push through.

My mother also showed me that greatness isn't passive. It's not an idea. Greatness is action. When she adopted my brother and me, she didn't know how to be a mother. She didn't know how to raise us, or even how she was going to feed and clothe us. What she did know, however, was that she loved us the moment that she saw us.

My birthmother, who I've never known, made Mamie Brown promise never to separate Wesley and me, and she didn't. I grew up with a lot of resentment toward my birthmother, but I released that burden when I read a quote by Kahlil Gibran:

"Our parents bring us into the world, but in the end, we are responsible for what we become."

He also said:

"Our children come through us, but not from us."

What this meant to me was that I was my own person. The person who gave birth to me didn't determine who I was, or who I was to become. I also realized that my real mother, Mamie Brown, chose to love us. She didn't have to.

She could have turned us away. She could have given us up. There were times when I'm sure she wanted to. I wasn't always the best kid growing up, but that beautiful woman stuck by my side and never gave up on me.

4

To this day, I carry that love and that determined spirit into everything I do. My mother loved and believed in me, and she believed in her ability to raise the two best boys and girl (my sister Margaret) that she could. I owe much of my success to the values that I learned from the great Mamie Brown, and I am proud to be her son.

Even with all of Mamie's love, though, I wasn't successful right out the gate. I've lived through hard times and times when I was convinced by others of my limitations. Thanks to great mentors like Mr. Leroy Washington, I found that these "limitations" existed only in other people's projections. For example, when I was young I was told that I had a learning disorder. Mr. Washington helped me realize that I should never let anyone convince me of my limitations.

In this book, I am going share more of my story. In this way, you'll see that I am not very different from you. I didn't grow up with advantages, but I took what I was given and used it to create greatness within myself and in my life. I believed in my goals, I believed in myself, and I stayed persistent. I didn't let other's opinions sway me, and I didn't take "No" for an answer. This is what got me to where I am today, and it will create success in YOUR life as well.

I am going to show you 12 laws that will change your life and help you to achieve your dreams. Follow the advice in this book and you will be **unstoppable**. No one and nothing will stand in your way anymore. I know this to be the truth because these are the principles that I've practiced in my own life.

These are the tools that I use every day to push myself further.

I want to be your mentor. I want to walk you through my success, and I want you to use the information that I share with you to create success in your life, no matter what that looks like.

Whether you want to be the best parent that you can be, or you want to start a Fortune 500 company, or you want to live out your dream of traveling the world, the lessons here will help get you there.

I say "help" get you there, because ultimately it's up to YOU to make the decision to be great. You see, greatness is a DECISION.

Let me repeat that:

Greatness is a DECISION.

YOU decide what your limits are, and YOU decide your level of success. You are responsible for the time that you spend on this planet. If you don't succeed, you have no one to blame but yourself. Where you are right now in life isn't the fault of your parents. It's not the fault of your teachers. It's not even the fault of your community!

Where you are right now depends completely on YOU.

I'm not saying this to put you down. I'm reminding you of your POWER. YOU have placed yourself in a situation in which you can't achieve greatness. YOU have decided to be less than what you could be - but you have the power to decide to be great. YOU have the power to choose success. YOU have the power to choose love.

YOU have the power to choose greatness!

In order to tap into this power, you need **HOPE**. You need to believe deep down that your dream life is there for the taking when you learn to persevere. I haven't always been successful, but I've always had hope. I've always known that if I kept plugging away and doing my best, I'd be successful.

I used to sleep on the floor of my office in Detroit. I used to sleep on the cold ground. But I kept my hope. I knew that it was only a moment in time, and that moment would pass. And guess what? I was right! I kept trying, and I found success.

People often give up after their first or second try. They give something a shot, and then because they don't get what they want immediately, they think that the opportunities aren't out there - that the job isn't available, that the position is filled, that it's an impossible field to break into.

6

You know what? SOMEONE is doing what YOU want to do! Did they get luckier than you? Did they stumble upon their career at a better time than you? Are they somehow fundamentally better than you? **NO**.

The people who are doing what you want to do - the ones at the top of your field, the ones you look up to - all started right where you are now. They all had their own trials and obstacles. The only difference between them and you is their persistence and their drive. They are willing to take the hits, they handle rejection and they work harder than anyone else around them.

Greatness wasn't handed to them. They CHOSE it.

I want you to find YOUR greatness. I want you to make the choice to be great, and I want it to reflect in every choice that you make moving forward. I want you to know, deep down, that you are <u>worth it</u>.

I also want to remind you that the clock is ticking. There is a number hanging over your head that's invisible to the human eye, but it's there. And you know what? It's always ticking down. The moments that you have left are continually slipping away.

That continual ticking is why you can't put this off. It's why you can't keep telling yourself, "Tomorrow..."

Tomorrow isn't real. Tomorrow never comes. There is only <u>RIGHT NOW</u>. The process starts in the present, and it only stops when you choose to stop. You need to choose to stop waiting for a tomorrow that never comes.

THE 12 LAWS OF SUCCESS

This is where the 12 Laws of Success come in. For the past 41 years, I have worked with hundreds of thousands of students all around the world. Some of them go on to create greatness in their lives. Others do not. There are 12 simple but powerful actions that those successful people take - but the unsuccessful do not.

If you learn and apply these 12 laws, then you will create greatness. It doesn't matter who you are, how much money you make, or what your interests are. With these 12 laws, you will absolutely be successful.

In this book, I am going to lay out these 12 laws and give you specific practices that will help you put them into action.

Some of these laws get to the core of who you are. You need to learn to listen to your heart. Your mind will help you to achieve success, but if you aren't listening to your heart, no amount of success will bring you happiness. You need to work toward the right goals by listening to what your heart wants. You then need to learn to enjoy the process. You need to love what you are doing, and you need to love putting in the work. If you don't, then you will never succeed.

Other laws in this book will force you to change. You'll need to drop your guard and release your fears. Your fears are holding you down, like the weight of the world on your shoulders. When you actually look closely at your **F.E.A.Rs**, you'll recognize that they aren't real. You've been straining your shoulders all of this time to carry something that simply isn't there.

Other laws will call on you to change your environment. You'll have to assemble a team of supporters. The right team will build you up, while the wrong one will tear you down. You have to remove toxic people from your life, and replace them with people who love and encourage you.

Still other laws are about what you give to others. I want you to become the type of person who lights up a room. I want you to strive to make the world a better place, and to create value in the lives of others. Everything you do and every decision you make should be from a place of good. You should always be striving to make the world a better place.

These all sound like lofty goals, but trust me, they are absolutely possible. Lesser people than you have gone on to achieve greatness because they understood the importance of these principles, which I will detail in the coming chapters.

This book is a blueprint for success, but it isn't success in and of itself. You must follow this blueprint and achieve your success for yourself.

You've already taken the first step. In picking this book up, you've made the decision to change your life. You've decided that you aren't happy where you are and where you are going. You've decided to change the course of your life, and you've decided to seek help. I'm proud of you.

Those who do not seek help will never receive it.

Now is the time to learn, and the instant you learn each lesson in this book is the time for action. Don't wait until you are finished with this book to take action. What if you stop reading halfway through for some reason?

If you are taking action as soon as you learn each lesson, I guarantee you'll be in a better place than you were when you started.

But read this book from cover to cover. Consider each and every word. I guarantee that no word is wasted. Everything in this book is here for a reason. This book is a tool to create happiness and success in your life. Utilize **ALL OF IT**.

Now it's time to learn how to change your life, and to put what you learn into practice. I believe in you. Mamie Brown's boy believes that YOU can achieve success and happiness.

<u>**It's time for YOU to believe as well**</u>.

LAW 1:
LISTEN TO YOUR HEART

I ask two things from you:

First is to actually read this book. The way you do anything is the way you do everything. If you can't get yourself to follow through on simply reading this book, then you can't expect to be able to follow through and do great things in your life.

Second is to be honest. This book will challenge you to take a hard look at yourself. If you truly want to succeed, then you need to be honest with what comes up in this book and in your life.

True honesty is hard. Throughout my career, I've faced moments where I've needed to take an honest look at myself and face some very uncomfortable realities. Even today, there are times where part of me wants to pretend that things are different than they actually are.

Mamie Brown taught me at a young age how to meet this challenge, and no matter how uncomfortable reality is, I force myself to face the truth. How? Remind yourself that it's ok. You aren't a failure if things aren't perfect in your life. In fact, the only way you can possibly fail is if you don't face the truth.

Because there's greatness within you, you WILL be honest with yourself as you read this book. To test your honesty, I want you to ask yourself a question. This question may take a little more thought than you first expect. Ready? Here it is:

Am I in control of my own life?

Now, don't just blurt out, "Yes." Really take a moment to let that question sink in. Let it take hold. Let it mull around inside of you for a moment, and really be honest with yourself.

If you think it through and you really do believe that you are in control of your own life, great! That means that you can do whatever you want with your life, right? That means you are doing exactly what you want to do, working the job that you want to work, traveling when you want to travel, and generally being happy with your current situation. Does this sound like your life?

If you aren't living a life beyond your wildest dreams, I want you to ask that question again:

Am I in control of my own life?

Now that question's meaning is probably starting to change a little bit in your mind. Reality may be starting to sneak in. Some doubt may be emerging. You may have changed that answer from a definitive "Yes" to an unsure "Maybe."

"Wait," you may be thinking, "Am I in control of my life?"

If you answered, "No" straight out of the gate, that's great! It's not great that you aren't in control of your life; it's great that you're being honest. You're telling it like it is. You've taken a quick inventory, discovered that you aren't happy with your life, and that someone else may be pulling the strings. While I'm happy that you understand this, it's not a great place to be.

Ask yourself this question every day until you know honestly that you are in control of your own life. This may take weeks, months, even years! The important thing here, though, is that you are aware of who is pulling the strings, and whether you are living your life or someone else is living it for you.

That's an odd thought, right? Someone else? Living my life? How is that even possible? When you give in to what other people want you to do, when you give in to the life that they want you to live, they're in control. They are the ones dictating your actions, and they are the ones making your decisions.

They are living your life while you're sitting in the backseat, tagging along for the ride.

There could be a variety of different people at the steering wheel, some that you may like, others that you may not. Your family may be driving you around, or it could be your friends, people on social media, society's standards, your cultural standards... Anyone might be at the wheel! If it isn't YOU, though, you aren't in control of where you are going.

You can complain about the direction of your life all you want, but until you sit in the driver's seat and begin to drive yourself, you aren't going to get where you want to go!

YOU need to take control of your own life. You need to find out what you are living for, and you need to get out and do it. You can't listen to what other people want from you and you can't allow them to decide what kind of life you're going to live. Even if they have your best interests in mind, they aren't you, and they don't know what will make you happy. YOU probably don't even know what makes you happy! Not yet at least...

In this chapter, we're going to discuss breaking through all of these different influences and listening to your heart. We're going to discuss how to get to the root of who you really want to be and what you were really put on this earth to do.

Read this quote:

"If you don't take control of your life, your days will be spent on the ends of strings pulled by someone else."

Now read it again.

"<u>If you don't take control of your life, your days will be spent on the ends of strings pulled by someone else</u>."

Let that sink in. Really let that quote get under your skin. Are you a puppet? Is someone pulling your strings? If so, it's time to cut those strings. It's time to go on an adventure. It's time to stop being a puppet and become a real person—the person you were always meant to be!

You have the power to be what you've always wanted and dreamt of being. You just don't know yet how to harness it. You've gotten lost in what other people said and expected. You've been lied to about your potential and you've been held down because other people are afraid of the great person you could become.

Why? Because success holds a mirror up to their failures. That's why people want you to follow the same path that they do. They either didn't dream big enough, or they were too scared to go after their dreams. Now they want you to think that you can't accomplish your goals either.

Well, guess what? **You AREN'T them.**

You are your own person, and you have the ability to create the life that you've always wanted. It's always been in you. It's time to let it out.

BREAKING FREE

Now you may be thinking, "Okay Les, I shouldn't just blindly follow what other people tell me to do. That's great. Now what?"

Well, now that you know what is causing you a great amount of unhappiness in your life, it's time to break free. It's time to take back control of your life, and it's time to start living in line with your real values and goals.

In order to be happy, to go to bed with a smile on your face and wake up full of energy and ready to start the day, you need to know what you want, and you need to be working toward it. This is the only way that you'll really be living your own life, for yourself, and not for anyone else.

Right now, if you are not fully engaged in your life, you might be living a life that is a little too safe. Don't get me wrong; logic is great. People need to use their brains. In fact, more people need to use their brains! Your logical mind, however, isn't the only place from which you should make decisions.

Where does your dream life truly come from? It comes from **the heart**. More specifically, it comes from listening to your heart. In order to live the life you were always meant to live, you need to dig deep inside. You need to be honest with yourself, and you need to find out what your heart really wants.

Your heart is an amazing guide because it isn't influenced by outside forces. It doesn't care what the "logical" decision is, and it doesn't care what your current influencers have to say about the life that you are "supposed" to live.

Your heart is connected to your purpose. It has a direct line with something more powerful, and it knows your role in God's divine plan. Your heart knows why you are here, and it breaks when you don't live in line with the life that you are supposed to be living.

That's why you get so sad when you think about how other people are living their dreams and living the lives that they want to live, but you aren't. It's because your heart knows what you are supposed to be doing, and you aren't listening to it.

Now, don't get me wrong. You need your logical brain as well. It can help you find opportunities and build a life that is in line with your heart and with God's divine plan. Together, the heart and mind are unstoppable!

WHAT DO YOU REALLY WANT?

To get a sense of how driven you are by your heart, I want you to think about three goals that you'd like to achieve, in three areas of your life. What is one personal goal that you'd like to achieve? Why is that important to you?

My first personal goal was to buy my mother a home, I am one of seven children that my mother adopted. I feel like Abraham Lincoln who said, "All that I am, and that I ever hope to be, I owe to my mother." She was a domestic worker on Miami Beach of the United States. She cleaned homes, and cared for children. We wore the hand-me-down clothes of the children that she kept.

She cooked for families, and we ate the food left over from the families that she cooked for. These were very kind and generous people. They would say, "Mami, whatever food is left over, you can pack it up and take it home to those children that you have adopted."

I used to walk around these big, beautiful mansions, and I'd say, "Mama?" She'd say, "What is it, Leslie?" "When I become a man, I'm going to buy you a big, beautiful home, just like this."

Was this a goal that came from logic? Of course not! In fact, it was a burden on my pocketbook. However, I was in line with what my heart wanted. I have never been more determined to make a dream a reality than this one. The day I bought my mother a house was one of the most fulfilling days of my life.

Now, I want you to think about your financial goals, growing your business, advancing your career, taking your life to the next level and so forth. I want you to think about the goals that you've set for yourself. Why do you want those things?

If they are small goals, they're probably not truly connected with what's in your heart. I found that most people fail in life, not because they aim too high and miss. I found that most people fail in life because they do what I did for much of my life, which is to aim too low and hit, and many may never aim at all.

Now think about your social contribution. What in your community will be different because you showed up? Horace Mann said, "We should be ashamed to die until we've made some major contribution to human kind."

If your goals are in line with your heart, then I have a simple message for you: "It's possible."

Now that you know that you should be listening to your heart, it's time to start discussing how you can get there.

GET IN TOUCH WITH YOUR HEART

You know that you need to listen to your heart, but you're probably wondering: "How do I learn my path? How do I listen to the universe and find my place in the divine plan? What is my path, and what do I need to do to get on that path?"

These questions can be difficult to answer, because when you try to think about them, you find that you're surrounded by noise. There is a hum all around you, a static like that of a TV that is always buzzing away in the background. Your computer is within your reach. Your phone is in your pocket or on your lap. There are people all around you giving advice, telling you their opinions, and generally talking your ear off.

With all of this noise, it can be hard to listen to your heart even though it's trying to break through to you all the time. You may feel that you are emotionally and spiritually drained. That's probably because your heart has been screaming for months or years, but you can't hear it over the noise of everything and everyone around you.

To break free of these outside influences and hear what your heart is trying to tell you, you need to find some quiet. You need to go somewhere that you can simply be, without distractions. There, you can practice different exercises that will open you up to what your heart has been trying to tell you all this time.

What happens once you get a moment of clarity and quiet is amazing. You begin to see things from a brand new perspective - one that you would never have seen before without taking a moment away from the noise of your everyday life.

Below, I've outlined a few different ways that you can open yourself up to the universe, open up your heart, and allow yourself to better see what God's plan is for you. If you practice these exercises, your true calling will begin to present itself, and you'll see what you've been missing all of this time.

JOURNALING

Do you own a pen? Great! You're a quarter of the way there. If you have a notebook, you're halfway there! If not, go out and get one. Once you have a pen and a notebook, all you need to do is start writing. What do you write? Anything that pops in your head.

Journaling is an age-old practice that has helped many great men and women to discover what has been right in front of their noses. It allows us to condense our days, reflect on our feelings, and store memories. It also allows us to learn from our past, and to recognize patterns.

Above all of that, journaling allows us to quiet the world around us and give our heart the podium. When you put a pen in your hand and you start writing without any real agenda, you find that your inner self takes over. Before you know it, you are writing things that you didn't even know you had in you, and you are learning far more about yourself than you would ever think possible.

You don't have to be a talented writer to journal. All you have to do is let the words flow. Don't stop to think too much, don't worry how it sounds or looks, and don't force it. Instead, let your mind wander; let your heart take the wheel and take you on a journey. Many people have made amazing self-discoveries simply by sitting down and letting the pen take off on the paper.

If you find that you're more comfortable typing, then type. Personally, I prefer handwriting because it forces me to slow down and think about what I'm writing. If you simply want to capture what happened in your day, great! Typing may be for you. If you want to take some time for silent contemplation and mindfulness, though, you may want to try handwriting your journal.

Either way, start writing every day. After a couple of weeks, read through what you've written. See what patterns emerge and what thoughts keep coming up. See what desires begin to peek through, and see what heartaches keep returning. This is a great way to discover what it is that you truly want, and what is holding you back.

MEDITATION

Another powerful way to open yourself up to your heart and the universe is through meditation. Meditation is a practice as old as mankind which has taken different forms throughout history. The reason it has lasted, even into modern times, is because it's a highly effective tool.

Meditation is like the skeleton key to your mind, your heart, and your spirit. It can open all of the doors!

While there are many different forms of meditation, you may want to focus on Zen meditation. This form of meditation helps to clear your mind of all of the noise and allows you to just **be**. Once you come out of this state, you'll find that you have a new level of clarity, and you'll be able to be more honest with yourself. You'll also be able to listen to your heart and what it desires.

For Zen meditation, you'll want to find somewhere comfortable to sit without distraction for an extended period. You don't have to sit cross-legged, and you don't have to sit on the floor. Just sit up straight in a chair or on your couch. Once you are comfortable, start taking deep breaths in, and deep breaths out. You can count in and out at first if it helps. In for five seconds, out for five seconds. In for ten seconds, out for ten seconds, and so on.

Once you feel yourself calming and your heart rate slowing, stop counting and just breathe. You may slouch a bit, and that's okay. Don't fight your body too hard, or you'll come out of your meditative state.

When you start to feel yourself slip away, your brain is going to kick into high gear. There will be a million different things vying for your attention, and those thoughts may get progressively more uncomfortable. That's all right. That's just your mind trying to stop you from accessing your heart. It isn't used to you letting go like this, so it is pulling out all of the stops to divert you away from a Zen state.

In order to stop it, you have to simply let it happen. That's right—DON'T fight it. The more you fight, the worse it'll get. Instead, acknowledge the thoughts or feelings that come up, and then simply let them go.

After a while, you'll get used to doing this, and your brain will stop throwing these things at you. You'll enter a state where the world slips away, and it's there that you'll find **true quiet**.

You may not get to this point on your first try, so don't get discouraged. Even if you don't let go completely, you'll find that when you come out of your meditative state, you'll still feel better than when you went in.

When you come out of your meditative state, allow yourself some time to readjust back into the world around you. Then take out your pen and notebook and start journaling. Just write down whatever comes to you. You may find that some of your greatest realizations surface once you've opened yourself up entirely.

FEEL DEEPER

Speaking of opening yourself up, you need to stop pushing emotions away. This isn't as much of a straightforward exercise; it is more of a general practice to incorporate into your life. Start feeling your emotions deeper, and explore them.

This all starts by giving yourself permission to feel emotions.

If you want to cry, go ahead and cry! If you want to laugh, laugh with your belly and your eyes. Laugh until you tear up. Laugh in a way that makes you look silly, and don't be ashamed. If you are angry, allow yourself to be angry (but don't allow yourself to be destructive).

Your emotions are there for a reason. They are trying to tell you something, and you have to listen to what they have to say!

You may be worried about over-emoting, and that's normal. Nobody wants to have a meltdown in public. Still, when you allow yourself to feel and you disassociate shame from your emotions, you'll find that they start to become quieter. Instead of building over time and exploding, you'll find that your emotions are more regulated.

When you allow yourself to experience your emotions instead of hiding them, they can come out in a controlled way. It's like a soda bottle that has been shaken up. If you open it quickly, it'll spray soda everywhere! If you open it slowly and release the carbonation a bit, though, it may fizz, but it won't explode.

Feel your emotions and live your truth. Don't be afraid of what you feel, and don't be afraid of why you are feeling these things.

MINDFULNESS PRACTICES

While there are many different mindfulness exercises that you can utilize, I want to focus on simply bringing yourself to the present moment.

We get so caught up in the future and we get so lost in our past that we lose track of what is happening in our lives moment to moment. This leads to a deep feeling of unease, and it wears away at our happiness.

In order to feel a sense of deep calm, and in order to approach life removed from our neurosis, we need to allow ourselves to be in the now, and be present.

A few different ways to focus yourself on the present are:

- Do something productive like cleaning the house. Pay attention to each detail, like each stroke when you are scrubbing the dishes. Smell the soap, and feel the pressure of the sponge on the dish.
- Pay attention to your breathing. Feel yourself breathe, hold it for a moment, and then breathe out.
- Notice something mundane, like the wood on your dining room table. Really explore it in a deeper way. Look at the different shapes, and follow the flow of the lines.
- Close your eyes and listen to the world around you. Listen to your air conditioner kick on, cars in the distance, or children playing.

The important thing here is to listen without judgment. Simply take in what is around you, and process it in the moment as it happens. This will help to clear your mind, and it will allow you to better focus on listening to your intuition instead of thinking about your laundry list of things that need to get done, the future, and the past.

Now, I Want to Ask You Again:

Are you in control of your own life?

If you use the techniques you've learned in this chapter, you will be more in tune with what your heart wants, and you will be able to hear what it is trying to tell you. That means you'll live your life in alignment with what you want, not just to please other people.

"If you don't take control of your life, your days will be spent on the ends of strings pulled by someone else."

Don't be someone else's puppet. Don't be society's puppet. Be your own person. Forge your own path, and do the things that you were put on this earth to do. Listen to your heart, and then use your mind as a tool to help you get what your heart wants.

Become more comfortable with silence, and find ways that let you block out the outside world. Really get to know yourself, and seek the path that was laid out for you. You have a purpose. In order to fulfill that purpose, you need to know what it is.

It all starts with quieting the noisy din around you - and listening.

Your heart will take over from there.

LAW 2:
LEVERAGE YOUR GIFTS AND TALENTS

Reading this book, you might be thinking, "Gee, he's been doing this his whole life. He must have known from an early age that this was what he was born to do."

But I didn't. I wasn't born knowing that I would be a motivational speaker coaching thousands of people to become their best selves.

The reality is that I went through a lot of trial and error to find my passion, and to discover what **talents** and **gifts** I was given by God. Lord knows that there were a lot of things that I thought I may be good at. I may have even gotten pretty good at them if I had stuck them out.

Instead, I found that not everything I tried was my true calling. We'll get to that in a moment.

For right now, I want you to get used to the idea that you may not be doing what you were born to do. You probably have a lot of untapped potential and you may not even be aware of it. Until you start working on developing your true gifts, you'll never feel comfortable with the path you are taking.

You see, while just about any skill can be learned, we were each given **gifts** at which we excel and have a true passion. Some of these are innate talents. You may find that you can run faster than other people, or you are particularly good at solving complex mathematical equations. If you nurture these gifts, you could put yourself on a path to true greatness.

You may find that you have a pure passion for something that, although you aren't naturally gifted for it, you are able to develop the **talent** to succeed in that field. I've met many people who were naturally gifted in ways, but who never went anywhere in life because they didn't develop or pursue their gifts. I've also met people who have a passion for something, and with years of pushing themselves to the limit, they built up their talent and surpassed the naturally gifted people.

In this chapter, I'll show you how to find the gifts that you were given and identify the passions from which you can develop the talent to succeed. I firmly believe that you are given a gift for a reason, but I also believe that you are given passion for the same reason. Once you discover your gifts, your passions, and at what you are (or can become) talented, you can start building the life that you were always meant to live.

One of the big issues that many people run into is that they don't know that they have untapped gifts and talent. They go through their entire lives working away at someone else's goal - and even get good at it. They can answer a phone and direct a call like nobody's business!

Still, their true gifts lie dormant, and they scratch away at the person's insides, like a dog scratching at the door when it's getting cold out. I once heard a minister say, "The wealthiest place on the planet is not in the Far East where there's oil in the ground, and it's not in South Africa where there are diamond mines. The wealthiest place on the planet is the cemetery. There you see potential never realized. There you find books never written. There you find ideas never acted on."

Your gifts want to be found. They want to be known. They want you to shake their hands and become best friends with them.

Beyond that, your gifts want to hang out with you. They want to develop a relationship. They don't just want to be casual acquaintances that you bond with deeply but only see a few times a year. They want to be involved in your life, and they want to help you to succeed.

Have you ever known someone who was perfect for you, whether romantically, platonically, or professionally? Whenever you spent time together, you clicked. It felt as if you were meant to be together; like you were somehow linked. As you got to know this person, this bond grew. Your relationship developed, and it became an asset. You found that this person was meant to be in your life and actually made you a better person.

Now, have you ever met these people, hung out with them a few times, and then blew them off? You had a great time, you could tell that you were supposed to get to know them and become close with them, but you didn't. God threw you a bone, and you chased it, sniffed it, and walked away.

Your gifts and talents are like this. God will present them sometimes, and it's up to you to develop them. Other times, you'll need to explore. Just like trying to find that special person in your life, you may need to get out there and meet a variety of different potential talents until you find one that fits. And as happens with people, you may find one and stick to it, trying to make it work even if it doesn't ultimately fit. These types of relationships, either with people or talents, are doomed to fail.

In this chapter, we'll discover how to identify your gifts and potential talents. I will also discuss how you can nurture and develop these gifts and talents, like a tree that you know will someday bear fruit.

You have innate gifts waiting to be discovered. They are like rare truffles that need to be sniffed out. Let's learn how to find them, and how to utilize them once they're found.

IDENTIFYING YOUR GIFTS AND TALENTS

Hiding deep underneath years wasted time and a life that someone else told you to live, lives your true calling. It got lost in that heap of years and misdirection, and you'll need to sift through everything that is piled on top to get to the heart of what you are supposed to be doing with your life.

You see, God has a plan for all of us. Each and every person reading this has an ideal life. This is the ideal life for you and for the universe's intention for you. There is a plan set out for each and every person, a map of sorts, but sometimes we get lost or lose the map.

Some people haven't even taken the time to look the map over. They've been following others who are just as lost as they are. Sure, your guide may know where he's going, but it probably isn't where you want to go. The guide is leading everyone to his own goals and you're simply along for the ride. You help to build the fires and search for food, but you never really get what you want. You don't get to travel the paths that you want to travel.

In order to know where you should be going, and follow the right path, you need to read your map. You need to figure out where you are right now, and then you have to figure out where you want to be. Only then can you set out on the right path.

There are a couple of different ways to discover your true calling. No matter how you find it, keep track of where you've been, where you are, and where you are thinking about going.

To do this, you need to start a **journal**. We discussed writing in a journal in the last chapter, and we discussed how it is a great way to listen to your heart and express yourself. We also discussed how it helps you to recognize patterns.

Journaling will help you to gain and maintain the awareness that you need to uncover your gifts and talents. It will also help you to see what keeps coming up, and it will help you to get a better view on what you have and haven't tried.

To find your gifts, you need to listen to your heart and you need to try new things ... things that you may never have tried before ... even things that you may be afraid to try. It's only by trying new things that we discover what we enjoy and what we don't.

By **listening to your obsessions** and **trying new things**, I strongly believe you'll be able to figure out where your gifts lie, and where you can build up your talents.

LISTEN TO YOUR OBSESSIONS

While not everything that you obsess over is what you are supposed to do with your life, nor something that you are particularly good at, it is often a great indicator of where your interests lie. You may discover gifts wrapped up in an obsession. That sounds a bit abstract, so let me bring it down to Earth.

Let's say you are really into fishing. Not just going fishing, either. You subscribe to fishing magazines, you watch fishing TV shows, and you go online to watch videos of people catching amazing, large fish. While you may not necessarily want to be the world's greatest fisherman, you may want to work somewhere in the field of fishing. You may discover that you have a gift for broadcasting, and the best way to utilize this gift is by discussing fishing on a podcast, TV show, or audio media.

On the other hand, your obsession may be your gift directly trying to communicate with you. You may become obsessed with helping other people, and this may be because your gift lies in making others happy. From here, you may find a career in community organizing, or working for a non-profit.

While your obsessions may fade, or they may not directly represent your gifts or talents, they could very well help to point you in the right direction.

TRY NEW THINGS

Another great way to identify your talents and gifts is by trying new things. If you are like most people, you are stuck in a cycle. You do the same things day in and day out, month in and month out. You become accustomed to these patterns and you find comfort in them. Note that I said **comfort**, NOT **happiness**.

If you are like most people, you probably don't try new things, and that's a shame! Without exposing yourself to new things, you can never truly know what you like or what you're good at.

It's time to break those routines and break free of the cycle you've locked yourself into. It's time to explore. Get out there and try all of the different things that you've always wanted to try.

Stop making excuses. Stop waiting to be thin enough, wealthy enough, or happy enough because you'll never get to that point of "enough." You'll keep waiting for everything to be perfect, and guess what? It never will be!

The stars won't align, the heavens won't open up, and God won't speak to YOU directly to tell you that now is the time to go travel the world.

You have to take the initiative. You need to jump in feet first. Even if you don't know everything there is to know, you'll learn. You'll be surprised to find out just how resilient you really are.

Go beyond - and try things that you never even dreamt of trying. For instance, you may have never considered taking an art class. You may be rooted in your job as an accountant, and all of the classes you took in college may have been based around numbers. You may have found that you were good at balancing a budget, but it's never really made you happy. Instead, you've gotten by, and you've stayed just comfortable enough to avoid rocking the boat.

Then you go to an art class and BAM - your life changes! Your goals change. You don't know what it is about picking up a paintbrush and putting it to the canvas, but you're hooked. Beyond that, you're good at it! You realize that all of that talent with math helps you to paint amazing circles and shapes. You understand geometry and angles in a way that other artists don't, and you can create amazing art using these gifts. You've discovered a new talent to master, and it comes from the gifts that you were given, but up to this point have misplaced.

Don't look at this as a negative. No matter how much time and energy you have invested into, say, your life as an accountant, it's never too late to make a change. It's never too late to open yourself up to new possibilities and change your life trajectory. Sure, you may need to start over. Sure, you may need to take some risks. But you know what?

All great things come from risk. I'm going to say this again, loud and clear:

All great things come from risk!

Greatness is a feat. It's a mountain that you need to climb. It's not an escalator, it's not an elevator. It's a mountain. You need to climb it. And with that climb comes inherent risk. I'm sure this isn't the first time you've heard that you need to take more risks, and I guarantee it won't be the last.

My point is this: In order to discover what you're good at, you're going to have to step outside of your comfort zone. Being comfortable all the time is boring, and you'll never accomplish anything great if you spend all of your life comfortable. Think about what would happen if you spent your whole life in bed. Would you be comfortable? Sure. You'd also be bored, and you'd never get anything done!

Get out there and try new things. Find your gifts and understand what talents need to be developed. Once you've gotten to this point, it's time to start developing those gifts and talents, and then build a life around them.

DEVELOPING YOUR GIFTS AND TALENTS

Congratulations for getting to this step. There are so many people who have never even explored what their gifts and talents may be. They haven't stepped outside of their comfort zone, and because of that, they are living a life that isn't in line with their true values or their true path.

Now, while identifying your gifts is admirable and definitely important, it doesn't stop here. You don't just get to say, "Well, I'm good at this. I guess I'm done." Just because you're good at something, or even gifted at it, doesn't mean that you know all there is to know about it. You aren't an expert yet, and in order to become an expert, you need to develop your gifts and talents into real skills.

Developing your gifts and really solidifying your talents requires the three actions outlined below. I am going to help you to take the rough sketch that you have of the life that you should be living, and help you to flesh it out into a beautiful work of art.

I'm not going to lie to you; this is going to take some work on your part. This isn't theoretical - it's active. It's a very real part of living the life that you were put on Earth to live.

When you finely hone your skills, you'll be unstoppable. You'll find that opportunities present themselves, and that you'll actually be in a position to take these opportunities. You'll become an expert, and because of that, you'll offer more value.

Once you are valuable, and you know what you're doing, people will want to work with you and help you achieve your goals.

So, let's get into the three most important things that you can do to develop your gifts and talents into real world skills.

1. Make a Commitment.

Big change means big commitment. When you set out to accomplish something, you can't go at it halfway. You need to be one hundred percent all in, and you need to build a regimen that will help you to reach your goals. This goes for any aspect of your life, including developing your gifts and talents. You have to be willing to develop yourself, and you need to take the steps that will help you get there.

I want to remind you what this book, ultimately, is all about—**personal development**. You are developing yourself, and in order for you to develop into something greater, you need to be committed to it.

Consider this example...

There's a man that we'll call Stan who is pretty overweight. When he visits his doctor, he finds out that it goes beyond his appearance. He finds out that his bad habits are causing problems with his heart, and if he doesn't make massive changes, he'll die.

This knowledge, of course, scares the daylights out of Stan, and he realizes that he needs to lose the weight and become healthier so he can live to see another year. He also realizes that this means dieting and exercising. These are two things that he's avoided like the plague. Still, in order to meet his goals, he needs to do these things.

So Stan makes the commitment. He lays out a regimen that includes a few days a week at the gym and a healthy meal plan. He then sticks to the commitment. He doesn't often deviate, but when he does he doesn't beat himself up for it. Instead, he keeps pushing forward, staying positive and staying on his path.

Stan goes to visit the doctor in a year, and the doctor is astounded. Stan's heart has fully recovered, and he is in the best shape of his life. He made a commitment, he put together a regimen and he stuck to it. Now he gets to live a longer and happier life.

Be like Stan. You might not need to lose weight to save your life, but you DO need to commit to developing your gifts and talents, and you need to put together a regimen that lets you do just that. When you put the regimen together, commit to it, and actually stick to it, you'll be unstoppable!

2. Identify a Skill and Work On It.

Decide that you're going the focus on developing your greatest skills. Don't overstretch yourself and try to develop a bunch of different skills at the same time.

Here's a quick story for you. A guy was a new owner of a baseball team that was in the basement of the league when he took it over. He went to the pitcher and he said, "What is your best throw?" The pitcher said, "I got a good curve ball and I got a good fast ball." He went on talking about his different throws.

"Tell me this. What is your best throw?" The pitcher thought for a moment. He said, "I've got a good fast ball." The new owner said, "That's all I want you to work on. Nothing else, just develop your fast ball." The next year, they went to the World Series.

Most people don't know what their fastball is. Most people go through life never discovering what their talents are. Most people never develop their talents. They have skills and abilities, but if you don't focus and nurture them, they will never serve you.

Your gifts can take you to many places if you develop them. Most of us don't like to do those things that come easy to us. I've always loved to talk to people. I decided, taking this advice, to develop my skills as a speaker. My gift has developed and developed, and it has taken me many places. You too have something that you brought to the universe, and if you decide to focus on it and develop it, then you will unlock an incredible future of success.

Let's say that you find out that you have a natural talent for music. You have a good ear for pitch, you understand how a song is written, and you have a strong understanding of tension and resolution.

Music is something that you are passionate about, and you know that if you throw everything that you've got at it, you can succeed as a musician. Now what skills do you need in order to be a great musician? Also, how can you upgrade these skills and work on them?

In order to be a great musician, you need to understand tempo, keys, scales, chords, and so on. You also need to know how the instrument works along with the dexterity to play it.

Great! Now you know what skills are needed. How do you develop them?

With music, it's all about practicing, and opening yourself up to new horizons. You may learn the basics first, like notes, chords, and scales, and you may practice those over and over until they are second nature. You may also get to the point where you can run the scales in your sleep, and you know the notes that build just about any chord.

Where do you go from there? Well, you start learning more advanced scales and chords. You start branching out into different genres of music, and you continue to develop your dexterity and knowledge. You keep working at it until you become an expert musician - and then you keep working at it some more!

3. Find the Right People and Surround Yourself With Them.

Now that you have a regimen in place, you've made a commitment, you've identified your skills, and you've started working on them, you're done, right?

Wrong! The next step is surrounding yourself with people who will help you grow and better understand your gifts, talents and skills. These people will push you. They will keep you on your toes. And they will never allow you to rest on your laurels.

These people will become your peers and your mentors. They will contribute to your growth in a way that you would have never been able to by yourself. They will introduce you not only to new aspects of your skills and gifts, but also to new aspects of who you are.

They will challenge your definition of yourself - from every angle.

We'll get more into surrounding yourself with the right people in a later chapter. It's a very important part of your growth and development.

When you take these three actions, it's impossible for your gifts and talents not to develop!

These three steps are game changers, and they will unlock potential in you that you didn't even know existed. You've got so much potential, but you still need to develop your gifts into real skills, or they will be wasted.

DON'T LET YOUR GIFTS GO TO WASTE!

You were given gifts from God. You have an ability that few other people have, and when you find it, you'll understand why you were put on this Earth. Things will begin to click, and working toward developing this gift into a set of skills that you can use will not only be enjoyable, but life-affirming.

If you hate what you are doing ... if you are working every day for a paycheck and nothing more, then you aren't living up to your potential. You aren't living in line with your gifts, and you aren't taking advantage of your talents.

Instead, you are a circle trying to fit into a square hole, and you are wasting all of your energy trying to fit into a hole that someone else fits into. You need to discover where you fit, where you belong, and what you are meant to do.

This is the path to happiness and success. This is the path to living a life beyond your wildest dreams.

When you do what you were put on this planet to do, life feels easy! That doesn't mean it won't take practice. It will. You'll need to hone these skills, and you'll need to work harder than anyone else around you to take your skills and build a life around them. But I'll tell you what - it's worth it.

The joy that you'll get from doing what you are meant to do is priceless.

So, get to it. Start figuring out what gifts you were given, unwrap them, and start playing with them. You'll find a new happiness and freedom that you never even knew existed!

LAW 3:
LET GO OF YOUR F.E.A.R.

So far, we've focused on how you need to follow your true path – the path your heart points you to. We've discussed a few of the barriers, like not listening to your heart in the first place and not knowing where your gifts and talents lie.

While those are important hurdles to clear, there's an even more daunting challenge which stalls many people. They hit this wall, they look up, and they see just how high it is. They immediately conclude that this wall is impossible to scale. They put down their grappling hook and their rope, turn around, and go home.

Do you know the name of this wall? It's written on it in blinking neon lights:

F.E.A.R.

That's right. FEAR is the number one obstacle that stops people from achieving their goals. It doesn't matter how talented they are. It doesn't matter how dissatisfied they are with their lives. People continue to trudge along living a life they weren't meant to live because they are afraid.

Many people are afraid to take the first step. They are afraid to break out of old habits. They are afraid of rejection, and they are afraid of failure. Whenever the mere idea of changing their lives comes up, they instantly shoot it down. They get uncomfortable and squirm around in their seats, just thinking about what it would take to change their lives.

I want you to honestly ask yourself if YOU are afraid.

Are your fears holding you back? Are they keeping you from reaching your goals? Are they keeping you from even exploring your options? If so, I want you to consider this acronym ...

- **F**alse
- **E**vidence
- **A**ppearing
- **R**eal

F.E.A.R. is up made of False Evidence which Appears Real. Your fears are rooted in a bias that you carry around with you, and that you can't move past. You may feel that you have evidence that you will fail. This false evidence has convinced you that you aren't capable of achieving your dreams.

You are afraid because you believe that you should be afraid. You may have been told that your goals are unrealistic. You may have even tried and failed in the past. Because of this, your belief system has changed. Now you believe that every outcome will lead to failure. Because one path didn't lead you where you wanted to go, all paths are going the wrong way.

Even worse, it's possible that someone gave you bad directions. They told you that the path to success was actually the path to failure - and you take their word for it!

So you settle. You take the path that's been tread over and over again. You know the path. The grass has been worn down to dirt from people walking on it so much. There are no branches hanging, no big bumps, no steep climbs.

This path is boring and predictable, BUT it feels safe. Everyone has told you that it's safe. You've seen many people take this path before you, so you believe it to be safe.

It sure seems safe. You follow the same boring path and you reach the same destination as everyone else, right?

Well, not always. The safe path also has a worst case scenario: You're following the safe path, and out of nowhere a bear emerges. You run.

You either run headlong into the woods or you run back to where you started.

You may take the traditional route because you are afraid of failure. We've discussed this route before. You go to college, you get a job at a big corporation, you do just enough to get by and then, out of nowhere, the bear attacks.

You get fired. You are sent either running into the woods, or back the way you came. This means finding a new job and starting over. Each time you do this, though, you become more tired - and it becomes more monotonous. You travel the same path again, seeing the same stuff, and hoping that you don't run into another bear.

Sounds like an awful life to live, doesn't it?

The reality is that THIS is the life you should fear! You should be afraid of following a boring path which leads to the same destination as everyone else. You should be even more afraid of following a path which, in reality, offers no guarantees - except the threat of having to start over.

I don't want this for you. YOU shouldn't want this for you. Instead, I want you to see false evidence for what it is - false. I want you to see that your fears aren't founded in anything real, and that the "safe" path isn't always very safe.

Most of all, I want you to learn how to put your fears aside and live the life that you were always meant to live.

Before we get into it, though, I want to tell you the story of a guy who wanted to change the world, but was afraid. I think you know who this story is about ...

When I was younger, I wanted to be a disc jockey. It was my dream job! I wanted to be on the radio. I wanted everyone to hear my voice. I wanted it very badly.

I did what any normal person would do: I put my dream aside. No, I'm just kidding! Actually, I landed a job at a radio station - not as a disc jockey, but I was still pretty excited. One day when one of the disc jockeys wasn't able to do his job, I jumped on the air. From there, I got the job as a DJ!

This story isn't about that, though.

I loved being a disc jockey, but what I was even more passionate about was social change. There were many changes going on in the world around me, and I wanted to support that progress.

I wanted to make the world a better place. So I spoke about it while I was on the air. At that point, I was told that maybe being a DJ wasn't enough for me; maybe I should run for public office. That idea seemed crazy. I didn't think I had what it took. I had no experience, and I would be running against an incumbent candidate.

Well, the universe decided that it was time for me to run as a member of the Ohio House of Representatives, because I got fired from being a DJ!

I was terrified to run for office. Not only was I terrified to be in office, which was a whole other set of fears, I was terrified just to <u>run</u> for office.

However, after a ringing endorsement from my mother and some campaigning, guess what? I won! I became a legislator, and I was able to start making the changes that I had always dreamt of making.

This is only one story of dozens in which I was scared to death. But I didn't let that fear ruin my chances of changing the world. I didn't let the false evidence sway me.

YOU shouldn't either.

Let's look at fear a little closer, starting with the most basic aspect: How we decide to respond to it.

HOW WE RESPOND TO FEAR

Everyone you know is afraid of something. It doesn't matter how fearless they seem. It doesn't matter what they've accomplished. Everyone has something that scares them. It could be a fear of heights, public speaking, commitment … anything.

Although we all experience fear, the way we respond to it is a different story. YOU choose how you respond to fear. You decide whether you have control over your fear, or if it has control over you.

It's likely that at this point in your life, you're giving in to your fears. That's okay. We're going to change that. But living a life of fear is leading you to make the types of decisions we discussed earlier.

Your fears are causing you to choose a safe path which may not, in fact, be safe.

It's time to change how you respond to fear - and it's time to be courageous. We'll discuss what courage really means in a moment.

First, I want to discuss the three Fs that come up when you are in a fear-inducing situation. These three Fs are hardwired into our DNA. They are natural responses that have helped to keep us alive throughout history. Although you probably aren't being chased by bears or tigers as often as our ancestors were, you still have these three Fs hardwired into your DNA:

- **Fight**
- **Flight**
- **Freeze**

Why do these exist - and what do they look like in today's world?

Flight

This is the mode that most people go into when they are met with some sort of discomfort or resistance. In nature, animals take flight or flee when approached by something that seems threatening. Similarly, humans today often run away from opportunities, challenges, and situations that take an extra bit of effort.

If you want to succeed in what you are doing, whether it is starting a business or starting a family, you can't take flight! Run away and you'll never get what you want from life. You'll spend your whole life exhausted from fleeing your problems, your dreams, and your goals.

Freeze

Another response that people often choose is to freeze. This response can be seen in animals. When frightened, they stand perfectly still before they take off. For most animals, freezing is a way to look less valuable, or to blend into the background. Sometimes they'll even play dead, in hopes that a predator will leave them alone.

This is a perfect analogy for many people's lives. They freeze! They stay in the same jobs, in the same relationships, and they fade away as they blend into the background. They try not to be noticed, and they hope that their problems will magically disappear, like a hunter who's lost sight of his prey.

Freezing is just as destructive a response as flight when it comes to trying to accomplish your goals and living the life of your dreams. Freezing means no progress. Without progress, you go nowhere. To be successful, you can't just sit around, frozen, waiting for things to happen. You have to be active.

Fight

The third F is the most dangerous. When confronted with danger, some animals will stand their ground. They dig in deep, and fight with everything they've got. Sometimes they fight because they're cornered. Other times they fight for their survival or for the survival of their offspring.

Win or lose, they give it their all.

If you want to succeed, THIS is the instinct to follow. You need to find that instinct within yourself to fight for what you want, and for what you know you deserve. You can't freeze up, and you can't run away.

I know it's scary. When you are facing adversity, it can feel like you are fighting a grizzly bear with a pocket knife! But believe me: You are stronger than you think. You are far more powerful than you could ever imagine. I want you to say this out loud:

I am powerful!

Now say it again, loud and proud!

I AM POWERFUL!

You have the power to fight, and you have the power to win.

"But what if I lose?" you might ask. The best part of this fight is that even if you lose, you come out stronger. You know why you failed, and you'll be stronger the next time you face that situation.

Luckily, you aren't literally fighting a bear, and losing your battles doesn't actually kill you. Instead, losing shows you how you need to adjust. Just as important, losing shows you that you've got **GRIT**.

Grit is one of my favorite words and one of my favorite attributes. Grit is the ability to push through. Even when they are uncomfortable, people with true grit will push through. They will look at insurmountable odds, and they will fight anyway.

People with grit give it their all. They run until their gas tank is empty, and then they get out of the car and walk the rest of the way. They go the last two rounds, even though every muscle in their body is telling them to give up. They face bankruptcy and still fight to see their dreams come true.

And when they lose, people with grit come back stronger and keep fighting for what they want.

I want YOU to fight. I want you to develop **true GRIT**. I want people to look at you and say, "That guy/gal is tough! They never back down from a fight!" In order to succeed, and in order to overcome your fears, you need grit, and you need the will to fight.

You also need:

Courage

Grit's best friend is courage. People who are courageous are able to face their fears, and they are able to run at them with everything they've got. You probably know some courageous people in your own life: Your father, your mother, your sister, your friend ... anyone.

Courageous people seem fearless. When they are hit with adversity, they push through it like it's nothing. They never back down from a fight, and they always seem so cool and composed.

Even if you don't personally know anyone who is courageous, you probably have some idols who are. They could be sports stars, musicians, political figures, or anyone - living or not - who has made a difference in the world. These people have become legends because of their courage. We look up to them because they always fight for what they want and believe in, even if they know they will lose.

Think about the ancient Spartans - the 300 soldiers who fought 10,000. They could have given up. They could have decided to lay down their arms and accept whatever fate was coming their way. I know that most people would have.

When you have an army of 10,000 killers staring you down, the natural instinct is to surrender - or run. But the Spartans did neither. They went down in history for courageously fighting this horde of men, even though they knew that the odds were stacked heavily against them.

How could these men stand there and face these odds?

When you think of the Spartans or anyone else courageous, you probably see them as being fearless too, right?

Wrong. The reality is that many of the most courageous people in the world are also scared out of their wits!

How could you not be? Imagine being a Spartan. Imagine facing down

10,000 men. You look around and see a few hundreds of your fellow soldiers, your friends, and you KNOW that most, if not all, are going to die. I don't care who you are; you're going to be scared!

It's okay to be scared. The difference between someone who is courageous and someone who isn't, though, is that someone who is courageous will fight through their fears.

You see, courage isn't fearlessness.

Courage is being afraid, and TAKING ACTION ANYWAY!

Some of the most courageous people I know were scared to death. They knew that they were risking their financial security, their future, their livelihood, their reputation, and just about everything to pursue their dreams. And you know what? They did it anyway.

Some of them failed. Actually, most of them did. I know I did. I haven't won every battle I've fought. I kept fighting though, and I continue to fight every day.

I'm still afraid of failure. The difference is, I don't let this fear deter me anymore. Instead, I look at my fears and I KNOW that I am stronger than them. I know that I can defeat them.

Don't be afraid of being afraid. Be afraid of giving up. Be afraid of failing to give it your all. That is the only real failure.

It's only when you give up hope and stop trying that you actually fail.

Have courage. Look at your fears, be afraid, and face them anyway. No matter what, you'll come out stronger and smarter than when you went in. You'll have learned a valuable lesson, and you'll have pushed yourself to your limits. You'll be able to hold your head high knowing that fear didn't stop you from working toward your goals.

When you mix this courage with true grit, you'll be unstoppable!

FEAR AND SELF-DEVELOPMENT

Fear is valuable. You've probably never heard that before. I agree that it sounds crazy. Other than keeping us from approaching poisonous snakes, how could it be valuable to be afraid of things?

Fear helps us because it shows us where we need to grow.

Bettering yourself isn't just a decision or a one step affair. You don't simply decide that you want something and poof - magically it's there. Getting what you want, becoming who you want, and achieving your goals is a process. It takes time, patience, and the ability to push past your fears to reach the next level.

Each stage of your development is going to come with its own fears attached. Just when you get comfortable and start to feel as if you've got the hang of it, something new will come up to scare you. Listen to this new fear; it's an opportunity to grow.

Remember: Growth isn't comfortable. Think back to your puberty. You grow hair in new places, you shoot up in height, you get acne, and your voice squeaks. It's awful! But without puberty, you can't develop into an adult. It's an annoying, embarrassing, and yes, scary process that leads to your development into a more fully formed version of yourself.

Pay attention to where your fears lie, especially when it comes to personal development. These fears will help to expose your weaknesses - the chinks in your armor. Once you know what your weaknesses are, you can start working on them. You can strengthen yourself where you are weak, and you can become a better version of who you are.

Here is an example that demonstrates the different fears that can arise when you are developing yourself. As I describe Chrissy, you'll see where her different fears appear and how these fears can help to identify the next steps she needs to take.

Chrissy is overweight. She knows that she needs to lose weight, both for her health and for her self-esteem. She used to be a lot thinner, and she knows that she's let herself go. She's decided that it's time to make some changes, so she makes the decision to start working out and eating healthier.

Chrissy's first fear concerns money. She's worried that if she spends a ton of money on healthy food and then doesn't eat it, she'll be throwing both the food and her money down the drain. She decides to take the risk, and she buys the healthy food.

Now she is confronted with cooking it. She's never been great at cooking and she often eats out. She's worried that if she cooks it wrong, it'll be inedible. She decides to look up some healthy recipes and she follows them as well as she can. The food doesn't turn out perfect, but it's good enough to eat. Over time, she gets better at cooking.

Her next priority is going to the gym. She's terrified! She knows it's going to be hard, and she's scared of finding out just how out of shape she is. She's also worried about being judged, and seeing other people watch her struggle in the gym.

She goes to a gym and gets a tour. Everyone is working out hard, and this intimidates her. She tells her gym guide how she feels, and he reassures her that new people come all the time and that she'll be fine.

Chrissy works up the nerve to go to the gym and has her first workout. It's tough, but she pushes through. No one judges her; no one even looks her way! When she's done at the gym, she goes home and cooks one of her healthy meals.

Her next fear is that all of this effort won't work. She is afraid that she will put in a major effort, but won't end up losing any weight. Still, she sticks with it. After a couple of weeks she weighs herself, and she's lost five pounds! She's on her way, and she feels great.

In this example, Chrissy was faced with a lot of different fears. Each time she faced one fear, others popped up. Still, she stayed strong. She braced herself with the courage to face each fear head on. Each time she overcame a fear, she developed further into the person that she wanted to become.

Fears can point you in the direction where you can grow. Find out what scares you, and face it. Not only will you be able to get past your fears, but you'll find that overcoming fears gives you a boost of confidence, proving that you are stronger than any fear you may have.

Be courageous, face your fears - and be gritty. Keep pushing through, no matter how hard it seems. You'll see exponential growth.

"There's Nothing to Fear but Fear Itself"

This is one of my favorite quotes. There is nothing as scary as what you make up in your own mind. When you start standing up to your fears, you'll find that they are a lot smaller than you would have imagined. Over time, your resolve becomes stronger, and you become more courageous. You start to look at fears as challenges to overcome, and you start to take pride in your grit and your ability to push forward, even when things seem impossible.

Remember what F.E.A.R. stands for: **False Evidence Appearing Real**. Your fears are usually based on a bias that is unfounded. They only appear real. In reality, they are obstacles waiting for you to overcome them, and they are growth opportunities waiting for you to take advantage of them.

It's okay to be afraid. It's not okay to run from these fears. Face your fears head on, and show them that you are stronger.

You are POWERFUL and you WILL overcome!

LAW 4:
LOCATE YOUR TEAM MEMBERS

I want you to stop and think about someone that you idolize. It can be anyone: A sports star, an actor, a businessperson, anyone who has achieved something great.

Picture that person in your mind. Picture a moment of greatness for them, such as the moment for which you best know them. It could be a rousing speech, an excellent monologue or the best song that you've ever heard. Bring that amazing picture to the front of your mind.

Now imagine everyone behind the scenes in that picture - the people who made that epic moment possible. It could be anyone from a manager to a makeup artist, agent, coach ... even a mother! All of these people contributed to that moment, and whomever you idolize wouldn't have accomplished what they did without that **team**.

Most people don't think about the team behind a celebrity, performer, or businessperson. They don't think about the people who put their heart and soul into helping someone succeed.

Do you know why you don't usually see these people? Because they aren't in it for the credit. They don't need the praise. They are either doing their job, helping someone that they care about, or both ... and that's enough. And you know what? The person you idolize knows how important their team is. They know that they wouldn't be anywhere without that team, and that's why they make sure to take good care of them.

Now, look at some people who used to be great. Think about someone that was once a great actor, rock star, or businessperson. Think about all of the things that they accomplished. Now, ask yourself, what happened? Where did this person go?

I would be willing to bet that the person you are imagining ran into some trouble with their team. Either they started taking their team for granted, or they got involved with people who took them for granted.

No, it's not always the case, but more often than not someone's head starts getting too big, and ego or greed takes over. This usually leads either to someone talented isolating themselves, or to someone greedy taking advantage of the person they are supposed to be helping.

Who you surround yourself with, and the team you put together, will ultimately determine your success or failure. No matter how talented you are, no matter how much drive you have, if you don't have the right people in your corner, your chances of making it are slim to none. Sure, you'll need to be self-reliant at certain points along the way, but even when you are working on a project by yourself, you still will need a team around you to give you the support that you need emotionally and spiritually.

Have you ever thought about something you wanted to do, and you talked yourself out of it? That's why it's necessary that we work with **Only Quality People**. Write that down. As you think about your goals and dreams, it's very important that you look at the people in your life and ask, "What is this relationship doing to me?"

MIT did a study that indicated that you earn within $2,000-$3,000 of your closest friends. When I heard that I got a lot of broke people out of my life! My mamma said, "Son, if you run around with nine broke people, I guarantee you, you'll become number ten." Dr. Dennis Kimball said, "If you're the smartest one in your group, you need to get a new group."

Cutting out all your broke friends is a little extreme and isn't even necessary. After all, as we'll talk about in this chapter, the people in your life can provide value to you in different ways.

Some of your teammates may be people you'd least expect. People like your friends, your parents, and fans of what you're trying to accomplish can give you the boost and confidence you need to keep going. I want you to keep this in mind when we get into team building. Your team may not look exactly the way you thought it would, but if you pay attention to the signs, it will be what it needs to be.

God wants to put the right people in your life to help you to achieve your goals and dreams. He knows who will keep you on your path. If you have your eyes and ears open, you'll quickly find out who has been put in your life to be a member of your team.

In this chapter, we're going to discuss the people that you are spending time with right now, and the value that they add. We'll also discuss putting together a new or revised team, and we'll discuss adding value to your team.

If you follow what we discuss in this chapter, you'll have the perfect team to accomplish your dreams. If you ignore it and try to go out on your own, or you surround yourself with the wrong people, you may find that success never comes … or when it does, it doesn't look the way you wanted it to.

Let's start by taking an inventory of the people who are currently adding value to your life. After that, we'll look at the opposite side of the spectrum: The people holding you back. Once you know who is in your life and why, you can start making the changes that you need to succeed.

YOUR CURRENT TEAM (THE VALUE GIVERS)

Start by asking yourself, "Who is adding value to my life?"

Some people in your life may be providing direct value. You may have coaches, co-workers, or business partners who are making your dream a reality. You also may have people who add value in a way that you can't quite quantify. This may be your friends or family, or anyone else cheering you on. Even if these people aren't directly contributing to your success, they are still helping you to achieve your goals.

Defining each type of value giver lets you take an inventory of people already helping you. I want you to see the people who are helping you get to the next level so that you can both invest more time and energy into those relationships and show gratitude for them.

Remember, no one is forcing these people to help you. They are choosing to help you along your path towards success. Don't take these people for granted, and don't treat them as if they will always be there. They may not.

Here are the different types of people who actively add value to your life:

The Cheerleader

The cheerleader is there for moral support, and to give you that extra push when you need it. Think about cheerleaders at a football game. They rev up the crowd as well as the players. They inspire confidence and help to keep the team's energy high.

You probably have some cheerleaders in your life: A significant other, your parents, your siblings, your friends, or anyone who believes in you and what you are doing. You may even have fans, and they may want you to succeed simply because they think what you are doing is amazing.

It's important to recognize these people, and to treat them with the respect that they deserve. True, they aren't providing you with specific opportunities, but they are there to help you keep your eye on the prize and your head in the game. They give you that extra boost when the chips are down. They are that encouraging pat on the back when it feels like all is lost.

I can't tell you how many times I've felt like giving up, and then someone who cared about me told me that I was better than that. I wouldn't be where I am today without those people.

Recognize the cheerleaders in your life, and cheer them on as well. Whatever they are trying to accomplish, give them the support that they need. You can boost each other up, and help to keep each other's morale high.

The Shoulder to Cry On

These team members are different from your cheerleaders. They are there for you when times get rough, and they are there to listen to you when you need to vent. Unlike the cheerleader, their job isn't to motivate you, at least not actively. Instead, they are there to help you decompress and process your feelings and emotions.

We all have times when our negative emotions get the best of us. We feel like we aren't worthy, we feel like we aren't good enough or like no matter what we do, we'll always fail. These feelings are all based on false evidence, of course. These are the F.E.A.R.s we discussed previously. These are your mind manufacturing reasons for you to give up, because that's what you've been conditioned to do.

When these times come, it's important to have someone who will listen. These people just listen. They don't strategize or tell you what to do. They may not even be very good at giving advice, but that doesn't matter. As long as they are good at showing up and can empathize with you, that's all that matters.

You may already have this person in your life, but you're afraid to go to them. You may feel that if you do, you're admitting failure. That's simply not the truth. Letting go of your negative emotions and processing your feelings is not only valuable, it's necessary. And just like any other necessity, processing your feelings DOES NOT make you weak.

Find that person in your life who will listen and give you a shoulder to cry on. In return, be that for someone else. It may be the same person or it may be someone else who needs help. However it manifests, be there for people when they need a listening ear and a shoulder to cry on. That's how you pay it forward.

The Strategist

Now we're getting to the people who actively help you produce. The strategist goes beyond the shoulder to cry on. Not only do strategists listen to what you are going through, but they actively help you make a game plan.

This may be a coach, a mentor, or someone who is going through or has gone through something similar and wants to help you out.

Imagine trying to find hidden treasure without a map. You're wandering around a deserted island for weeks with no idea where the treasure is. Then someone walks up to you with a map. They say, "Here. See that 'X'? That's where you need to go. And this is how you get there." Now you have a solid lead on where to go.

Sometimes your strategist will be wrong. Sometimes the X may be five feet too far to the right or the left. Still, they will help you get a lot closer to reaching your goal than if you tried to do it by yourself.

Listen to your coaches, your mentors, and other people who have been there and want to help. You don't have to do everything they say, but at least be respectful and listen. Even if you only use one piece of their advice, that's still more value than you had.

The Partner

This is the person with the most vested interest in your success. You may have partners in relationships, businesses, or anything else that requires effort. Your partner can be a mix of all of the team members we've discussed - a shoulder to cry on, a strategist, and more.

Mostly, though, the partner is the person who wants you to succeed the most because they will ALSO succeed. This isn't a selfish thing. If you are married, and your spouse is happy and successful, guess what? YOU'RE more likely to be happy and successful as well!

Partnership means a commitment. It means joining together and working at something with the thought and energy that neither of you could achieve by yourselves. Partnerships can be a beautiful thing, if you don't get in the way of yourselves. Allow your partner to do what they do best, and do your best as well. This will lead to both of you winning.

Invest the Time

Make a list of the people in your life. Yes, ALL of them. Now, go through and find the people who contribute the most to your life. Spend more time with these people. Invest more time and energy into building these relationships, and be there for them when they need you. We'll get into that more in a little bit.

Once you have that list of people, I want you to look at the people who didn't make it onto your list of contributors. These people are most likely your detractors - your Value Takers.

YOUR CURRENT TEAM (THE VALUE TAKERS)

Now that we've looked at the people who are giving you the most value in your life, I want to flip things around. I want to look at the people who are draining you: The takers. These are the people who sucking up your resources, zap your energy, or otherwise lower your spirit.

These are the people who tell you that you can't make it, the people that always have their hand out and/or the people who are coasting through life. They are complainers, and they push their negative energy onto you until you give up.

They may or may not be doing this on purpose. Some people are just raised to act this way. Others are jealous. They can't stand to see someone doing well, because it shines a mirror up to them and shows them the bad things about themselves.

Whatever the case may be, you need to eliminate the value takers from your life. There may be some value takers who you can't eliminate (we'll get to them in a moment). But get rid of everyone who is an expendable value taker! They are only holding you back and wasting your precious energy.

Here are some examples of value takers:

The Complainer

There are some people that are so negative, they could walk into a dark room and begin to develop. Nothing is ever good enough. They always want more. If they don't want more, they want everything easier. They don't value hard work, and it's always someone else's fault that their life is hard.

These people do just enough to get by, and then get mad that they don't have more. They want the house, the car, the computer, the surround sound system and the plasma screen 4K television, but they don't want to do anything to get these things. They don't want to work harder. They don't want to set goals, and they don't want to take risks. In reality, they may not even want the things that they say they want. They may just want to complain.

Complainers not only bring negative energy into your life, but they try to get you to subscribe to the same nonsense to which they've sold themselves; they want you to complain as well.

I once was in line at a fast food restaurant, behind a woman who was getting impatient. She scoffed, she shuffled, and she looked at her watch. The line was pretty long, but I could see why. The restaurant was severely understaffed, and I could see the people behind the counter, running around, working hard to meet the needs of their customers.

She turned around and looked at me. Do you know what she said? "I can't believe this is taking them so long! What is wrong with these people?"

I was stunned. I looked at the poor people busting their butts to get the customers' orders out, and then I looked at her and said, "There's nothing wrong with them. They're working as hard as they can." I wanted to add "Maybe the problem is YOU!"

I'll tell you what, this woman could not have looked any more angry at my response! In her mind, it was okay to complain about something no one could do anything about, and she wanted me to buy into her negativity. Even more, she wanted me to get angry at the people who were trying their hardest.

When she saw that I wasn't buying it, she got angry. That's okay. She can be angry. That's her right. It's also my right not to buy into her anger, though. I don't have to be a complainer. I can see the situation for what it is, and I can wait in line or take my business elsewhere.

Stop letting complainers dictate how you feel about a situation, and never let their negativity drag you down.

The Do-Nothings

Do-nothings differ from complainers in that they don't say negative things all the time. The problem is that they don't do or say anything positive. They just keep trudging along, doing nothing of note with their lives.

The do-nothings won't try to bring you down, but they won't boost you up either. They simply exist. They don't contribute much value, and they take as much as they're warranted. Avoid these people, if for no other reason than the possibility that their do-nothing attitude may infect you.

If you start to feel that you can just get by in your current situation, and you see people who have given up on their dreams, you may start to believe that doing nothing is okay - or even a good idea.

Trust me, it's not. Don't be a do-nothing, and stay away from them.

The Haters

This is a fairly modern term (at least it is for me) and it's a great one! Haters are people who are trying to hate what you are doing. These people used to be called naysayers. Haters exist almost solely to tell other people that their goals aren't possible. They want everyone to know that their dreams are dumb, and that they need to give up. These are the **most toxic** people in your life!

Unlike other groups, the haters will actively try to get you to quit. They want you to give up because it gives them validation. They see someone who cares, someone who is trying to live a good life, and it forces them to realize that they aren't doing anything with their own lives. They aren't happy, so they feel that other people shouldn't be happy either.

I really feel sorry for these people. I feel sorry that their primary motivation in life is being negative. What really stinks about them, though, isn't just their negativity. It's their wasted potential. These people have passion and they try hard, but their passion is to bring other people down! If they took that energy and put it toward something positive, I really believe these people could accomplish great things. I don't believe it enough to hang out with them and try and change their mind, though.

If someone is committed to being a hater, let them hate. That is, let them hate from a distance - as far away from YOU as possible!

The Vacuums

I call this next group "the vacuums" because they suck up everything in their path without giving anything back. Unlike a real vacuum, though, they don't serve a purpose. There isn't a symbiotic relationship with these people. Instead, they sit around sucking up resources.

They bum and borrow. They take and never return. They are the ones living with their parents well into their adult life, and they refuse to do a hard day's work. They owe everyone money, and they never intend to pay it back.

A vacuum will suck you dry if you let it. A vacuum the ultimate form of taker. Don't let these people into your life.

WHAT ABOUT PEOPLE I CARE ABOUT?

Now that we've discussed the negative people in your life, you're probably wondering what can be done about certain people in your life who you love and/or can't eliminate because they are family members, family friends, or co-workers. What do you do with these people?

The answer: Limit your time with them. Remove yourself whenever possible, and when you are around them, avoid talking about anything more than small talk. Talk about the weather. Talk about sports - even though they may complain about it raining and their team losing! Talk generally about anything that doesn't give them a chance to rant about how awful life is.

These people may come around in their own time, but it isn't your job to force it or to fix them. Look out for yourself and your happiness, and don't let these people drag you down.

I want you to keep this in mind:

Know who you can count ON, and who you should count OUT.

Know who will boost your team up, and know who will bring your team down.

BUILDING YOUR DREAM TEAM

You might remember the original "Dream Team," the 1996 Chicago Bulls basketball team. Jordan, Pippen, Rodman ... they were the perfect team, and it showed. Throughout the 90s, the Chicago Bulls were practically unstoppable. A lot of people say it's because of Michael Jordan, but in reality, it was the whole team that won championship after championship.

I want you to build your own dream team, with all of the best players that you have available. If you don't have a large pool from which to choose, or if you are missing a player with a specific expertise, you may need to go out and find these people.

In order to find people to build your team, you may need to start making some connections. For a lot of people, I realize this may sound easier than it is to actually do. You may be shy, or you may not know where to go to meet the right people for your team.

But you can do it. Here's how:

MAKE CONNECTIONS EVERYWHERE

I'm a firm believer in introducing yourself to people who are around you. This includes everyone from people in line in front of you to people standing next to you in the elevator. If they're within three yards of you, say "Hello." Who knows? It may be your next best friend ... or a potential client.

The more you practice this, the better you'll get at it. Before you know it, you'll be saying "Hi" to everyone!

Spend Time in the Right Places

They say that if you hang out in a barbershop long enough, you're bound to get a haircut. Although this is usually used as a negative, I think it can also be stated in a positive way as well. For instance, if you spend time where a lot of other successful people are, you're bound to become successful!

Find out where people in your field go, and make a conscious effort to not only go to these places, but to introduce yourself to people there. You may find a new partner, coach, mentor, or someone who is gives you great advice or introduces you to someone who helps you reach your goals.

Make a Social Friend

If you aren't a social person, consider making a social friend. If you don't immediately network with anyone else, try to find someone friendly who is able to make introductions. A social friend can help you meet other people and put together the perfect team.

Always Have "Win-Win" In Mind

The last thing I want to mention about building your dream team is that you should always have win-win relationships in mind. In other words, don't be a taker without being a giver too. Be willing to give your own kind of value to anyone from whom you take value.

Some people may not want anything in return for their help. The value that they get is the satisfaction of knowing that they helped someone else. For most people, though, value is expected to be returned. Even with people who don't expect anything to be returned, you should pay them back in some way when given the opportunity.

The more win-win relationships you have, the better your chances of success are, and the stronger your team you will be.

Update Your Roster

Now it's time to do an inventory of your current team and update your roster. Have an idea in mind about the type of people that you need on your team, and start working toward putting your dream team together. Remember: Always be willing to add value. Your team should be built on win-win relationships.

Alone you will fall. Together, you will see success that you never would have dreamt possible.

LAW 5:
LIFT UP YOUR MIND WITH
SELF DEVELOPMENT

I want to tell you something. You may not believe me, but I want you to mull it around. I want you to think about it throughout the next few days. I want it to impact you, and I want you to remind yourself multiple times a day. I want this to be part of who you are.

Ready?

<u>YOU have GREATNESS in you</u>!

Yes, YOU.

You have the power to take this life by the reins, and lead it in whatever direction you want it to go. You have the ability to lead the charge to a better life, and you have the ability to truly be great.

You may look at your idols, or other great men and women, and you may think that they are a different breed - maybe even a completely different species! You may think that there's no way they could be human beings - normal ones, anyway.

Well, guess what? They are. They are made of flesh and bone, just like you. They bleed, they sweat, they dream, and they get scared. They have gone through tough times, they worry, and they sometimes think that they aren't good enough. The difference is that they push through it. They remind themselves of their greatness, and they continue to grow.

<u>Great people don't stop at greatness</u>. Great people are always developing and always growing. People who have accomplished great things know that they aren't finished. Their greatness doesn't end at a trophy, a prize, or a few million dollars in the bank.

Instead, they continue to grow and they continue to develop. Sometimes this means getting better in other areas of their lives. Other times it means becoming the best at what they do, and even then, growing further. Greatness is reaching for the limits of human potential, and continuing to grow from there.

Did you know that since the 1800s, people thought it was impossible to run a mile in under four minutes? Many people would get close, but the belief at the time was that four minutes was the marker of human potential. No one could beat it.

Then, in 1954, Roger Bannister ran a mile in under four minutes. People couldn't believe it. Incredibly, only forty-six days later, John Landy did it as well. Since then there have been more.

People thought that breaking the four-minute mile was impossible ... until someone did it. There are perceived limits to greatness, and then there are the real limits. Self-development will help you to push beyond your perceived limits to reach your full potential. Even when you think you've reached it, though, you can't stop there. You need to keep pushing forward and reaching for new heights.

In this chapter, we are going to discuss self-development, from developing the right self-development habits to pushing yourself beyond your limits. If you truly want to achieve greatness, you'll continue to push. You'll reach beyond your limits, and you'll keep developing yourself until the day you die.

Let's get started on turning self-development into a habit for you.

SELF-DEVELOPMENT AS A HABIT

One of the most important things you need to do is to create good habits. We are creatures of habit. We do the same things day in and day out without even realizing it.

Some habits will help you grow and develop, some habits will help you maintain, and other habits will wear you down over time. I want you to take a look at your habits objectively, and see what kind you have.

Some of your habits will probably remain at maintenance level, and that's okay. For instance, you probably aren't going to get a whole lot better at showering or brushing your teeth!

Other habits, on the other hand, can be built upon and changed, with items added or subtracted. I want you to look at your day and find where there's time to add self-development.

Self-development needs to become a habit, just like brushing your teeth or showering. Self-development should be something you do often enough that you realize when you skip it, and you miss it. I know that when I go a couple of days without working on developing myself, I feel a void. I feel a nagging that tells me that there's something I should be doing ... and there is!

If you feel like you are booked, try cutting time out of something else that you are doing, or work self-development into another activity. For instance, if you watch TV for a couple of hours a day, take a chunk of time out of that and spend it on personal development instead. If you listen to the radio on the way to work, buy an audio book that helps you to grow and develop. Listen to an inspirational audio, a podcast for self-development, or an audiobook that makes you more efficient at what you are trying to accomplish.

However you work it into your day, make sure that self-development is part of your life - a daily habit. I know that you can find some time in your day to better yourself, even if it's only half an hour.

Make self-development into a habit that you don't intend to break, and over time it will become an important part of your life.

READ 30 PAGES A DAY

41 years ago, I made a promise to myself to read 30 pages a day. It's one of the simplest commitments I've ever made and it has created unbelievable results for my life. One of the most beneficial practices that you can incorporate into your life is reading 30 pages or more a day.

I know 30 pages seems like a lot, but that's part of the point. You need to get used to being outside of your comfort zone, and you want to get better at doing things that you may not want to do.

Now, when I say to read 30 pages a day, I don't mean 30 pages of a romance novel. You should be reading 30 pages of self-development. It may be a book geared towards boosting your self-esteem, a blog about starting your own business, or a magazine that teaches you how to get into better shape. Whatever the material that you choose to read, make sure it is something that will help you in your journey to become a better version of yourself.

30 pages a day adds up. When you do the math, that means you're reading a full-length book every week to week and a half. If you are reading at that speed, you can read about fifty books a year! At that rate, it's almost impossible to NOT become an expert at whatever part of yourself that you are trying to develop.

You can mix up the reading as well. For instance, you may want to learn more about becoming a better public speaker one week, and then learn about being a better parent the next. That's fine, as long as you are actively bettering yourself and working toward your goals and your dream life.

I want to challenge you to push yourself: Read 30 pages a day for the next three weeks. That's it. 21 days. Don't skip a day, and don't make excuses. If you do, go back to Day One. Once you read 30 pages a day for 21 days, I want you to think about all that you have learned. I also want you to think about the habit that you have built.

You may not realize it, but after three weeks of reading every day, it'll be as easy and natural as brushing your teeth. It won't feel like a chore anymore. But don't worry about that. For now, I want you to read those 30 pages a day for the next three weeks. Then I want you to reflect on it.

I guarantee that reading 30 pages a day will change your life. It will expand your mind for what is possible. You will develop a spirit of optimism and hurl yourself towards greatness.

PUSH OUT OF YOUR COMFORT ZONE (MENTALLY AND PHYSICALLY)

Some of the biggest barriers we face are the ones we build ourselves.

This is important, and it bears repeating:

Some of the biggest barriers we face are the ones we build ourselves.

It's amazing. We are all experts at getting in our own way. More than other people, more than luck or chance, more than anything, WE get in OUR OWN way. WE stop ourselves from taking advantage of the opportunities that present themselves, and WE are the ones who are too scared to make the changes that we need to make.

We discussed F.E.A.R. earlier, but just to remind you: F.E.A.R. stands for **false evidence appearing real**. Our comfort zones are built out of this false evidence. Our comfort zones are actually the epitome of false evidence.

I'll tell you why. Our comfort zones are the allotted space that we give ourselves to grow, and we build them out of false notions about what is or isn't possible. What we find impossible, we are too scared to face. So, our false evidence manifests into these comfort zones that we live our lives in.

And you know what? Our comfort zones are comfortable. We are safe there. We're also bored. Nothing very exciting happens in a comfort zone. Comfort zones are also pretty small, which means that there's no room to grow.

In order to progress, develop, and succeed, we need to break out of our comfort zones. We need to deconstruct these artificial barriers that we've built, and we need to take a bold step further than we ever thought we could. THAT is where growth lies. THAT is where success lies. And THAT is where true happiness lies.

There are two comfort zones that most people find themselves in: **Mental** and **Physical**. In order to develop and grow, you need to push yourself beyond your perceived boundaries both mentally and physically.
I know it sounds tough. I know it sounds scary. But you have to be stronger than you believe that you are.

Believe me when I say: You are stronger than you think you are.

YOU ARE POWERFUL.

Before we get into the two different types of comfort zones, I want to share an amazing quote with you:

"Great things never came from comfort zones."

This is a life changing and life affirming belief. Nothing great has come from someone sitting around believing that everything is exactly as good as it will ever get.

Greatness comes from people striving for more than what is, and instead looking at what can be.

Let's look at the two different kinds of comfort zones and discover how you can break out of yours.

PHYSICAL

I believe it's easier to push beyond your physical comfort zone than it is your mental one. You may think that I'm crazy to believe that. Maybe it's been a while since you've done any more exercise than climbing the stairs! Or you may think that you are limited because of your age or a handicap.

Believe me: You are not limited by anything other than your self-imposed comfort zone. I've seen men in wheelchairs doing pushups. I've watched videos of the oldest female weightlifter pushing through her routine like it's nothing.

We've all seen videos of people with no legs running and competing. If you haven't, go on the Internet now and watch some because they're awe-inspiring. They're impressive and tough to watch. Not because we feel pity for them ... but because we feel pity for ourselves. These people overcome incredible odds while we make excuses based on the artificial comfort zones that we've created.

I want you to challenge yourself, and I want you to push beyond your perceived physical limits. I want you to do something that's hard, and I want you to keep doing it until it becomes easy.

I saw an amazing quote the other day, and it changed the way I looked at exercise:

"It hurts now, but one day this will become your warmup."

WOW. Tell me that idea isn't inspiring!

I've spoken to some great athletes, and they testify to this. Not every great athlete started great. Some started out of shape, and worked hard until they could compete at the highest level. What they started with, what pushed them beyond their limits, they now knock out in the first ten minutes of their workout. It really is their warmup!

Like everything else, it's all a matter of perspective. If you believe that you can only walk around the block once, you'll only walk around the block once.

Remember, people believed that no one could run a mile in under four minutes.

Push yourself physically, and you'll not only grow physically stronger, but you'll grow mentally. You'll become much more mentally tough, and you'll begin to believe in the great things that you are able to accomplish.

MENTAL

Here's the hard part. Here's the part that makes most people want to throw in the towel. You need to build mental toughness if you want to succeed. You need to be able to see the barriers in your life, and you have to know deep within yourself that you can knock them down.

You need to know that your comfort zone is all in your head, and you need to stop listening to that voice that tells you that it's time to quit, because more often than not, that voice is WRONG.

A lot of this has to do with perspective. You may feel that you have bad days. We all have bad days.

The thing is, you don't have to have a "bad" day. Instead, you can have a character-building day! You can look at your day and think, how has this day made me stronger? What have I learned that I didn't know before? What is the takeaway here?

Once you change the way you perceive things, you reroute the part of your brain that tells you how things are "supposed to be." You start pushing against your perceived barriers, and you start to grow in ways that you never expected were possible.

Your success hinges on how mentally tough you are, and how willing you are to break through your discomfort.

I'm going to tell you right now that you never get to a point where you're fully comfortable. If you do, then you know that you are resting on your laurels, and there is more work to do!

I want to challenge you to start working toward finding out where your comfort zones are, both mentally and physically. Once you identify these comfort zones, I want you to start stepping outside of them. You don't have to make a huge leap at first. Take a step outside of your comfort zone and walk around. See what it's like. Once you get comfortable, start tearing down the barriers.

When you find that a new comfort zone arises, do the same thing, but do it quicker and more efficiently. You'll eventually get to the point where you are able to quickly recognize your comfort zones, and steamroll your way through them!

Comfort zones are stagnation, and **stagnation is the death of progress**. Keep pushing forward, and keep working toward your dreams.

START YOUR DAY RIGHT

I am a big fan of routines, and I believe that in order to grow and develop, you need to have the right routines in place. These routines should start first thing in the morning, when your brain is first starting to kick into gear.

I bet a lot of you start your morning in a way that is either neutral, or even counterproductive. You probably roll over in bed, and the first thing you do is check your phone. Who called? Who sent me a message on social media? Who liked my posts? Who emailed me?

Others may start the day by turning on the TV and soaking up the latest gossip, the sad affairs of the world, or droning, mind-numbing shows that are built to sell you shampoo and fast food during their paid ad time. This may feel like you're doing something (heck, you may even feel informed), but in reality you are just starting your day at a handicap. You're either taking in negativity, or you are numbing your brain.

Instead, your mornings should be packed with self-development!

I know this sounds overwhelming. I totally understand not being a morning person. Still, habits will help to reform your wasted morning hours so that by the time you walk out the door, you've already done something productive.

Start by rolling out of bed, making your bed, getting on your knees, and saying thanks. Pray to whomever you believe will listen, and tell them how grateful you are to spend another day on this side of the grass. Ask for the strength that you need to get through the day, and ask for the courage to continue with your path toward personal growth. Tell God about the things that you are thankful for, and ask for the strength to take the burdens that he has given you.

After that, turn on something uplifting. It could be upbeat music, it could be your favorite inspirational podcasts, or it could be one of my tapes! Whatever it is, make sure it's something that will pump you up and give you the energy and motivation to get through your day.

If you want to take it to the next level, get up extra early and get a little exercise in. This goes along with breaking through your physical comfort zones. Start the day with a walk, a jog, jump rope, push-ups, squats ... whatever you can handle. Get the blood pumping and get your energy flowing.

Finally, make your commute to work productive. Listen to motivational speeches, listen to audiobooks, or say affirmations out loud to yourself in your car on the way to work. Try to make every minute of your morning count.

This will set the tone for the rest of your day, and will help you focus on the tasks you need to complete to improve your life.

ALWAYS BE GROWING

If you're in sales, or if you've ever been in sales, you've probably heard the expression "always be closing."

I'm going to ask you to do something slightly different. I'm going to ask you to always be growing. I want you to look at your life as an opportunity to always be pushing beyond your comfort zone, and developing yourself.

You have so much greatness in you, it's unbelievable. Still, you need to start believing the hype.

You need to start buying into the idea that you ARE great, because it's the truth. It's reality.

You are the embodiment of greatness, and you're keeping yourself chained up in a cage that is your comfort zone. Take off the chains. Break through your comfort zone. Be who you were meant to be.

Always be growing, always be pushing, and always be developing into the unstoppable force that you were meant to be.

LAW 6:
LEAVE ALL NEGATIVITY AND TOXINS BEHIND

Back in my early days of trying to become a disk jockey, I went to apply for a job in Miami Beach. Milton Butterball Smith was the program director at a local radio station.

"Hello, Mr. Butterball, how are you, sir? My name is Les Brown, sir. I'd like to be a disc jockey."

"Young man, do you have any journalism in your background?" "No, sir, I don't."

"Do you have any experience in broadcasting?" "No, sir, but I visualize myself being on the air every day, sir. I practice. All I want is a shot. Just give me a shot."

He said, "No, we don't have any job for you." I was devastated with rejection. I went back to my mentor Mr. Leroy Washington and I said, "Hey, Mr. Washington, they said no." He said, "Don't take it personally. Most people are so negative they have to say no seven times before they say yes. You've got to be hungry. Go back again." I said, "Yes, sir."

"Hello, Mr. Butterball, how are you, sir? My name is Les Brown, sir. I'd like to be a disc jockey." "Young man, weren't you here yesterday?" "Yes, sir." "Didn't I tell you no yesterday?" "Yes, sir." "Then why are you back today?" "Well, sir, I didn't know whether or not somebody was laid off or somebody was fired, sir." "Nobody was laid off or fired, now, get on out of here!"

I came back the next day. "Hello, Mr. Butterball, how are you, sir? My name is Les Brown, sir. I'd like to be a disc jockey." "I know what your name is. Weren't you here the last two days?" "Yes, sir." "Didn't I tell you no the last two days?" "Yes, sir." "Then why are you back today?" "Well, sir, I didn't know whether or not someone got sick or someone died, sir." "No one got sick or died, no on was laid off or fired, no, don't you come back here again."

I came back the next day. Talking loud, looking happy, like I was seeing him for the first time. I said, "Hello, Mr. Butterball, how are you?" He looked at me with rage. He says, "Go get me some coffee." I said, "Yes, sir."

That's how I got a terrific opportunity as a disk jockey in Miami Beach. It would go on to change my life. Let me ask you something: if I had faced that first rejection, gone home and talked to someone who said "wow Les, I'm sorry that happened to you. You should probably try doing something else with your life," would I have gone back again? Would I have gone back the third time, or the fourth time? Of course not!

Like we've talked about throughout this book, what you think about, you bring about. The energy around you, positive or negative, plays a huge role in that.

TOXIC ENERGY

If you look around, you see opportunities for negativity all around you. Notice that I don't say that you see "negativity" all around you, but rather **opportunities** for negativity. Your life is a series of choices, and these choices can lead you down a positive or a negative path. Your life is also guided by your perceptions; the way you see the world can dictate the kind of world that manifests around you.

A lot of people see the world as a negative place. All they see is corruption, greed, sadness, and anger. Most of the people that they know are just getting by, and never seem to have any luck. Their lives have been a series of missteps, and they are constantly waiting for someone to pull them from the rubble, dust them off, and offer them a career in a lucrative field.

When these people see that this isn't happening, they complain. They put all of their energy into convincing others that this is the nature of the universe; that the world is out to get them, you, and everyone you love. I feel terrible for these people.

I was only a few bad decisions and a few negative thoughts away from this very same path. The difference is that I chose positivity. You can too.

What if you are already on a negative path? What if you see the world as being built of haves and have-nots? What if you feel that the odds are stacked against you?

I want you to know that it's okay. There is **HOPE**. All you have to do is hold on to a little hope, nurture it, and watch it grow. As it grows, you need to clean out the weeds around it. Clear out the negativity that is zapping the life force of this hope and sucking up all of its resources. You need to tear these negative influences away, and make room for a full garden of hope to grow in their place.

In this chapter, we're going to clear your garden of weeds. I want you to be able to grow and cultivate HOPE, to move beyond the toxic beliefs and people who are holding you back from reaching your full potential.

Trust me. No matter where you are right now in life, there is always room for growth. And no matter how stuck you feel, there is always a path that will lead you to your dreams.

I know that there is hope. My life wasn't perfect either. There was no straight shot for me to get to the top easily. I was given limits on what I could accomplish. I was told "no" plenty of times. And I was led to believe that my worth was far below what it actually is.

But look at me now. If I had let those negative people, negative thoughts, and negative beliefs guide my life, I'd be miserable! I never would have accomplished my dreams, and I certainly wouldn't have written this book.

YOUR ENVIRONMENT AFFECTS YOUR GROWTH

I found my way through the darkness, and I want to help you find your way out. To do so, you must understand the power of your surrounding environment. If your hope is being choked by surrounding weeds, it will die.

Can a flower grow through concrete? Of course not. You can't grow with the burden of a negative environment surrounding you.

Your environment helps to determine your growth. That doesn't mean that you must stay in a bad place if you were born there. Plenty of people who were born poor and without resources have pushed beyond and accomplished great things. These people didn't do this by sticking around their original environment, though.

Instead of trying to force the entire world to change for you, you'll need to get out from under the concrete and go where your growth can flourish.

To put it in more practical terms, if you are in a bad environment, you probably won't accomplish great things there. Change the people, places and items around you so that they reflect where you **WANT TO BE**, rather than where you were or where you don't want to be.

If you are poor, you don't want to stay in a poor area that doesn't have any opportunities, surrounded by poor people who don't have any dreams of moving up in the world. You need to surround yourself with people who are doing well, and you need to spend more time in places that foster this mentality. Even if circumstances prevent you from physically move out of your geographic area right away, you CAN "move out" mentally and spiritually with the tools below - until you find a way to actually relocate your residence.

Are you surrounded by an environment that's limiting you?

Here's how to identify and eliminate different factors such as negative people, media, mental toxins, and physical toxins from your life - and start replacing them with hope.

NEGATIVE PEOPLE

There are few things in this world which can affect you as much as the people around you. While it's important not to let other people's opinions determine what you do with your life, it's hard to keep your head up and to stay positive when the people around you are bringing you down.

I've known my fair share of negative people. As a boy, I was told that I had a learning disorder and that my potential was limited. Being so young, I believed it. It wasn't until an amazing teacher of mine told me to ignore what I'd been told and that I WAS capable of learning, that I was able to progress.

So in my case, a negative person knocked me off my path very early on. Luckily, a greater man came along and restored my faith in myself, allowing me to shed those shackles and grow.

I've been told time and again about my limits ... and time and again I've proven the naysayers wrong. And you know what? I stopped caring about what those people thought and said, and I stopped surrounding myself with people like them. Instead, I chose to hang out with winners.

When you stick with winners, can you guess what you end up doing? That's right. You end up winning.

You need to identify the negative people in your life and get rid of them. If you can't get rid of them, at least reduce their influence over you and reduce your exposure to them.

Think of these people as being very sick with a bad cold that you don't want to catch. Stay away!

I get that there will be people you can never fully remove from your life. It may be a family member or a co-worker who tries to keep you down. While you can't get away from them entirely, you CAN stop asking for their opinion. You CAN stand up for what you believe. And you CAN surround yourself with so many positive voices that their meek little negative voice fades into the background.

You don't have to listen to naysayers, and you don't need to be around them. Instead, find places and people who push you forward instead of holding you back.

Be proactive and live a full life. Live full, die empty. Go to activities that attract people who are trying to make their worlds larger and better; people who are trying to cultivate the hope in their gardens. Mingle, make friends, and shoot each other ideas. Lift each other up and be constructive. Challenge the people around you, and ask them to challenge you as well.

If you're the smartest person in the room, you're in the wrong room. Grow together with positive people, instead of allowing negative people to drag you down.

NEGATIVE MEDIA

We are conditioned to be fearful.

We are always looking for the next thing to scare us, and most people get lost in negative media sources. Not long ago, people got news from a newspaper or the evening TV news.

These days, 24 hour news channels, the internet, and social media bombard us with world news, celebrity news, national news and more - every moment of every day - in real time. Notifications go off to let us know that a story is unfolding. Our social media feeds prioritize stories that other people are reacting to, often negatively. Sometimes it seems impossible to escape the barrage of information!

The problem is that we're getting more information than ever, but becoming less educated. Instead of challenging our beliefs and expanding our perspective, we get news from sources that simply reinforce our existing beliefs and make us feel outraged at people who don't share our beliefs.

In addition, because the news is all about drama and conflict, it tends to reinforce a negative worldview. The funny thing is, there's just as much positive news out there as there is negative news. The positive isn't always as interesting, though, and people love controversy and the charge of adrenaline that comes with it.

I want you to do something, and I'm dead serious: Go to your social media feeds, and unfollow all of your friends, pages, and groups that post predominately negative items.

Also, stop cut down on the amount of mindless news you watch.

In fact, it would be really smart for you to go on a media cleanse. For a couple of days, don't check social media, don't watch TV, don't read the paper, and don't check your email (except for work). Remove yourself from all the noise and distractions. Allow yourself some peace and quiet. Read a book, get caught up on work and listen to some of your favorite music. Go for a walk, get some exercise, and meet up with some friends. Make positive decisions and avoid the negative.

You will be amazed at what this small detoxification will do for you. All of a sudden, you'll have much more positive energy. You'll also find that you are far more productive.

On the first day you may experience a "negative media withdrawal" and be itching to check your favorite website. Push past this withdrawal, and you'll see just how rewarding an experience a media detox can be.

When you return from your detox, be very selective of the media that you choose to use. Be mindful of the kind of television, movies, and even books you read. Make sure you're reading and watching news that is actually adding to your understanding of the world rather than giving you an empty jolt of validation.

Consider what you are feeding your plant of hope. You can't feed it anything toxic if you want it to grow. Keep your media intake upbeat, and unsubscribe to negativity and the naysayers.

MENTAL TOXINS

Most people's heads are like attics: Dusty and full of clutter! Every once in a while, we need to go up there and clear out the cobwebs to get things in order. We need to get rid of stuff that we don't need. We need to put stuff away that we'll need for later. And we need to find and take down the stuff we need, but haven't been using.

To see the world clearly, you need to remove the toxic elements that have infected your brain and messed with your perception. In order to do this, you need to practice meditation and mindfulness.

We discussed these topics earlier, but I want to circle back around to them in the context of introducing positivity and removing negativity.

This isn't simply about calming yourself. This is about using meditation and mindfulness to explore deep within yourself, identify the negative, and cut it out like a tumor. That's right. I want you to think about the negativity that infects you as if it is a tumor. Not only is it unnecessary, but it's sucking the life out of you. You need to cut it out in order to heal.

PRACTICE POSITIVE THINKING

In general, throughout your day, try to practice positive thinking. Whenever you see a potentially negative situation, try to look at it from a different perspective and in a new light. Think about the good that will come out of the situation, and don't let the darkness take away your light.

Positive thinking does not mean putting your head in the sand. The kind of positive thinking I am talking about is more like *powerful thinking*. You are giving yourself the power to shape your current situation in the way you want.

PHYSICAL TOXINS

Physical toxins come in the form of poor nutrition and poor exercise. Physical toxins result in extra weight, disease, poor sleep patterns, pain, and many other physical symptoms.

Your body is a temple. Think for a minute about the way that you should treat a temple.

What would your place of worship look like if it resembled your body? Would the paint be peeling from the walls? Would there be trash all over the ground? Would there be dust collecting on the pews? If you really stop to think about your body in this way, I can guarantee that you'll want to make a change.

The easy way to live our lives is to allow our temple to collect trash, dirt, and dust. The easy thing to do is to let it fall apart. When the doors start coming off their hinges, we allow it. When a pipe breaks, we ignore it. But this easy way also leads to a temple that no one wants to visit, including ourselves.

In order to keep your temple in shape, you need to clean up after yourself, you need to put work into fixing what needs to be fixed, and you need to use only the best tools and materials to rebuild what's broken.

What does all that mean? It means you need to exercise and you need to eat better.

Are you the kind of person who eats fast food more than once per week? (I don't mean one day per week. I mean one meal per week.) Do you drink soda? Do you skip out on drinking water? Do you consume more sugar in a day than three people need? Are most of the things that you eat cooked in grease and covered empty calories? If so, you need to make some changes.

In order to be the best person that you can, you need the right fuel. Eat healthy food with plenty of nutrients. Give your body what it needs to fuel your greatness.

On top of eating right, you need to exercise. This isn't a fitness book, so I'm not going to go into a detailed workout routine. But start getting your heart rate up. Find different exercises and classes that you find enjoyable, and go to them regularly.

When your eating habits and your exercise habits are on point, you'll find that your body and your mind both run better. Your mind, body, and spirit are all linked. In order to succeed, you need to care for all three.

TAKE A STAND

When you remove the negative influences from your life, you are telling yourself and those around you **MY LIFE MATTERS. MY LIFE HAS VALUE. MY LIFE IS IMPORTANT.**

Your life is a masterpiece, and it's being built one stroke of paint at a time. You may feel that if you make a mistake, it ruins the masterpiece. In reality, all you have to do is wait for the paint to dry. Then, you can paint over that mistake with something new and something better.

Don't let mistakes and the negativity that they bring drag you down. You're better than that.

We discussed the toxins in your life. We discussed how to eliminate them and cleanse yourself. We discussed the garden of hope, and how to pull the weeds from that garden if you want your hope to grow and flourish.

Now it's time for action. Remove the negative people, media, and other influences from your life, and replace them with positive people and things. You'll be healthier, happier, and much more successful.

You'll give yourself the foundation you need to create greatness in your life.

LAW 7:
FOLLOW THE SUCCESS TRAILS THAT HAVE BEEN PAVED BEFORE YOU

So far we've talked about what you need to succeed. Now let's talk about **who** you need to succeed.

As we discussed earlier, success is a team effort. Every success story has multiple supporting characters. If you try to climb the mountain of success by yourself, you're probably not going to make it. Even if you do, it'll be much harder than it needs to be.

You also know that each different member of your team has an important role in pushing you forward and helping you overcome obstacles. But there are certain members who are truly crucial to your overall success:

Mentors.

Finding and attracting mentors is the game changer.

This chapter will show you exactly how to do that.

Yes, You Need Mentors.

Greatness is passed down by successful people to others who will eventually take their place and even surpass them. Mentors guide their mentees, and in turn, those mentees create their own success and become mentors to new mentees. It's a positive cycle that allows us to move forward as a society.

I've had many mentors throughout my life who have changed the way I see the world. I wouldn't be the speaker I am today without all the amazing speakers from whom I learned. I wouldn't be the kind of success I am today without amazing mentors like Leroy Washington, Dr. Robert Schuller, and of course Mama Brown. I've also been a mentor, and can tell you exactly what separates my successful mentees from unsuccessful mentees.

Even if you're the smartest person in the world, you're going to have a rough time without mentors. Trying to become successful without mentors is like trying to discover calculus on your own. You'll spend the rest of your life trying to figure out stuff that smart people have experienced and can explain to you in a couple weeks.

It doesn't matter how talented you are either. The best athletes need coaches to point out flaws in their game. The most successful businesspeople join mastermind groups to get feedback and new ideas. The best chefs read cookbooks to take their craft to the next level.

Follow the success trails of others, and you'll unlock limitless success. No matter what road you're on, having a mentor to guide you around the potholes and the detours will get you to your destination faster and easier than without one.

People have been brave enough to carve out a path ahead of you, and if you are able to follow in their footsteps, you'll find the path to greatness. This isn't to say that you have to become them. As we've discussed, you are your own person with your own unique talents and gifts.

Rather than copying your mentors, you'll learn from them to become great in your own way. Mentors are there to lead us where we need to go, and give us guidance as we progress.

"But Les," you may be saying, "I'm not a motivational speaker. How can I find a mentor?"

You don't have to have the same goals as me to achieve the same levels of success. Every field imaginable, from computer programming to teaching English, has people who have achieved greatness and gone beyond the call of duty. They have inspired the people in their lives and they have done great things.

No matter what field you're in, you can find a mentor. There will be someone out there who has blazed the path before you, and wants to help show you the way.

If you get involved in what you love and really surround yourself with it, you'll find success stories. Those success stories will point you to potential mentors who know the path, and may be willing to show you the way.

I'm not going to lie and tell you that every successful person wants to be your mentor. I'm also not going to say that those who want to be your mentor won't expect anything from you. Mentors want strong students who are willing to listen, take risks, and appreciate the help they are given.

If you are willing to be a great student, you can find someone successful in your field to be your perfect mentor.

In this chapter, we talk about how to find a fantastic mentor who can help bring out your greatness. You'll also learn how to be a great student, so great mentors will want to keep working with you. This knowledge will let you find and keep great mentors who can reveal the map you need to be successful.

Let's start with what makes the perfect mentor.

THE PERFECT MENTOR

A mentor isn't just any random person in your chosen industry. It isn't even any random successful person in your industry.

While many people may appear to be ideal mentor prospects, further investigation may show you that they won't lead you down the right path. They may be miserable in their field, they may not want anyone to mentor, or they may just be terrible mentors.

When you are looking for the right mentors, look for three main attributes: They should have more experience than you, they should be willing to help, and they should love what they're doing. We'll go through each of these in more detail.

Before we go through each of these attributes in detail, I want to tell you a story about a mentor who dramatically changed my life and perhaps more than anyone besides Mama Brown gave me the courage to reach for my dreams. You've heard his name already: Mr. Leroy Washington.

Mr. Washington was an English teacher at my high school. I really looked up to him. He held himself with poise and he was well known in the community. Everyone liked and respected him, and when he spoke, they listened.

When I was in eleventh grade, I attended a speech that Mr. Washington gave to the graduating seniors at my school. It seemed that the speech he gave was for ME.

It was the speech that I needed to hear and it sticks with me to this day:

"As graduating seniors of Booker T. Washington High School, I want you to know that you're blessed and highly favored. As you go toward the future, begin to know that you have greatness within you. If just one of you here begins to envision yourself as being blessed and highly favored to reach your goals ... if just ONE OF YOU captures the essence of what that means - **that you have greatness within you and a responsibility to manifest that greatness** - you can make your parents proud, you can make your school proud, you can touch millions of people's lives and the world will never be the same again, because you came this way."

He got a standing ovation. When he left, I ran out to the parking lot to meet him. I told him that I wanted to work with people, and I wanted to buy my mom a home. That was my dream. I asked him if it was possible. He said, "It's possible, Mr. Brown."

As he began to walk away, I stopped him again and I said,

"I'm the one, sir. You remember me, sir. I'm miss Mamie Brown's son. I'm the one."

He took me under his wing and he inspired me. I actually began to wear his hand-me-down clothing even though they were too big for me, because I wanted to be just like him. I told him one day that I would surpass him, that I'd be an even better speaker and even more famous ...and I did. I know that I made that man proud. The values that he instilled in me will follow me for the rest of my life.

What are the three traits that great mentors like Mr. Washington have?

MENTOR TRAIT 1: THEY HAVE PLENTY OF SUCCESSFUL EXPERIENCE

The first thing you'll want to consider is how far along down the line your potential mentors are. The perfect mentors have experience under their belts. They've been there and they've done that. Their advice comes from a wealth of experience, and it is priceless.

While anyone who's further ahead than you can give you great advice, choose someone who has really made it, or has a track record of helping others make it. This is someone who has made it all the way to the top of the mountain, maybe multiple times, and can show you the way up. The worst thing you can do is pick someone who's only halfway up the mountain and doesn't know how to make it the rest of the way.

Look into what your mentor has accomplished. Look at his or her history of accomplishments, and see if they've mentored other people in the past. See where these mentees are. Did they go on to accomplish great things? If your potential mentor has a good track record, then it'll be easier to trust that they can do the same with you.

MENTOR TRAIT 2: THEY LOVE WHAT THEY'RE DOING

While people may be successful at what they do, they may not truly love doing it. Many times they have sacrificed a part of themselves in the process of becoming successful, and this missing piece has tainted their success.

Miserable people aren't the types of mentors that you want in your life. They may lead you down the path to success, but that path may lead you through the same pitfalls that they hit. This could discourage you, or worse, you could push through and become miserable too.

Sure, you can learn lessons from miserable people. I've learned a lot about sales from miserable salespeople. However, I would not advise investing time and energy to build a relationship with someone like that.

In my experience, people who don't love what they do can be downright toxic when they're mentoring. And remember, you don't want toxic influences in your life.

You need to love what you do, so your mentor needs to love what they do as well.

MENTOR TRAIT 3: THEY ARE WILLING TO HELP

Write this down: **You need to know whom you can count on, and whom you can count out.** That applies to a mentorship relationship just as it applies to any other relationship.

You may find that some people like **the idea** of doing something more than actually doing it. You may find someone who is further down the line and knows what they're doing, but they aren't really interested in helping others. Some people may tell you, "No," outright ... others may say, "Yes," but then never provide the guidance that you need.

You don't usually pay the people who mentor you. That's why your mentors have nothing tying themselves to you other than a desire to help you. If that desire diminishes, or if they decide that the mentorship isn't working for them, they can drop you at any time.

Of course, part of this relationship is putting in the work and being a good student. Even if you are, however, they may decide for any number of reasons that they don't want to continue mentoring. That said, you will be surprised how much time and energy a mentor will invest in you if you are a good mentee.

Once You've Found the Right Mentor ...

... it's time to build a strong relationship with this mentor. To do this, you want it to be built on the basic win-win principle.

BUILDING A WIN-WIN RELATIONSHIP

Like everything else, if you expect to receive, you're going to need to give a little. This applies to mentorships one hundred percent. Even if someone is mentoring you for free, they want to get something out of the relationship. That something is your success - and your ability to pass the gift along.

That's why, to create the perfect mentorship, you need to be open to making the experience just as great for your mentor as it is for you.

I've mentored a few people in my day, and I settle for nothing less than greatness. Your mentor should be the same way. They should expect great things out of you, and you know what? They deserve that. They deserve to watch their hard work and effort pay off.

How do you build a win-win relationship with your mentor so that they want to keep helping you, and so that you can feel good knowing you've made them proud?

Let's discuss your ability to be open to taking feedback, along with how you can pay it forward. These are the two expectations that any good mentor will have, and you should be eager to deliver them.

TAKING ADVICE AND TAKING ACTION

Nobody likes to talk to a brick wall. If you don't believe me, go outside and start talking to one. See if it listens to you.

Just like a brick wall, some people don't listen. You can give them advice until you're blue in the face, and they still keep doing their own thing. If this is you, don't even waste a potential mentor's time.

You need to be open to what your mentor has to say. You need to be willing to listen to make it worth your mentor's time. I know you may have your own way of doing things, and it has gotten you as far as you are. But if you sincerely want to take yourself to the next level, you need to be willing to listen.

Beyond that, you need to be willing to ACT.

Some people are great listeners. They'll take notes, they'll nod earnestly, and they'll say all the right things. When it's time to pull the trigger, however, they sit around doing nothing. They stare at the target, expecting it to hit itself.

This is SO frustrating to mentors! Mentors know that you have all of the needed knowledge, but for some reason you are just sitting on that information. They are providing you with what could be thousands of dollars' worth of advice, and you are choosing to do nothing.

Well, guess what? When another issue comes up, or when you finally decide to move forward, they may not be there anymore. Mentors are usually busy people, and if you aren't taking their advice, they'll simply leave you behind.

Not listening and not following the advice of your mentors is rude, disrespectful, and a waste of their time. I'm sorry to be so blunt, but it's true. You need to understand that there are hundreds or even thousands of people out there who could benefit from their personalized attention.

You should be willing not only to listen, but to create value. You need to take in everything that they teach you and put it into practice. If some of it doesn't work out, that's fine. Adapt. You'll get more hits than misses, and it'll be worth your time.

Once you've listened and you've taken action, you'll start to become successful. Over time, you'll reach the top of your field. When that time comes, it's time to start giving back.

GIVING BACK

As we progress and become successful, we become more powerful. You probably recognize this quote from a famous superhero...

"With great power comes great responsibility."
This is true in all aspects of life. In mentorships, our power carries with it the responsibility both to our mentors and to others to pass along the knowledge that we've been given. Don't be a miser. Don't just sit on the amazing information that you have been taught.

Part of the joy of being a mentor is watching the student become the teacher. It's genuinely exciting when your student starts coming to you with questions about how to help others achieve success. It shows that they appreciate what you have done for them and that they want to give back by passing it along.

You owe it to your mentor, you owe it to others, you owe it to the universe, and you owe it to yourself to give back. You were given a gift, and now it's time to pass that gift along to someone else.

Be willing to help those who are struggling, or who need some advice to get over a hurdle. If you can, find a student of your own, and help him or her rise to the top. True, not everyone will pan out and not everyone will listen, but when you do find that perfect student (and you will), you'll see that it was all worth it. You'll share the joy that your mentor felt when passing the information along to you, and the cycle of growth and development will continue.

Both Parties Should Get Something Out of It

Mentorships are a two-way street. Keep this in mind when someone decides to spend their time helping you out. Time is money, and they are giving you a gift that is more valuable than cash or gold: They are giving you knowledge.

Thank them by taking the advice that they're giving you, and when the time comes, pay it forward!

HOW TO CONNECT WITH GREATNESS

I know that some people may seem untouchable. You may really want them to mentor you, but you may not know how you can speak with them. For me, there were a few different factors that helped me make needed connections and find the mentors that I wanted.

Consider the following methods. These all helped me network with some of the most respected public speakers in the world, and allowed me to find some world class mentors.

GO TO EVENTS

One of the single greatest ways to network is to go to events and meet people in person. While some events are larger than others, and your chances of meeting a big name star is lower, you still have the opportunity to network. If you say, "Hello" to enough people, and let them know your mission, eventually you'll find someone who knows someone.

Events also allow you to meet people you may not have considered as potential mentors - until you find out what they've accomplished. I know that there have been times that I've shaken someone's hand not knowing who they were, and later on they ended up being of great help to me.

Keep in mind that at these events, the person you look up to may be swamped. Be brief and be honest. Let them know what you are after, and ask if they are willing to help. Don't be rude about it, but be straightforward. Don't waste their time beating around the bush.

Events allow you to meet people you would never have met otherwise, other people looking to accomplish the same goals, as well as potential mentors. When an event in your field is coming up, get tickets and go!

BE PERSISTENT

I want to tell you a story. This will allow you to better understand the level of persistence that I expect from you.

I really wanted to be on the Dr. Robert Schuller's show, which was a Christian television show. I knew that if I could get on there, it would be an amazing opportunity for me. More people would hear my message than ever before, and I would be able to establish myself as an expert. So I went around for about three years telling everyone that I met that I was going to be on the Dr. Robert Schuller Show.

They'd say, "Is that right?" and I'd say, "Yes, it is."

Then they'd say, "When are you scheduled?" and I'd say, "I'm not sure. I haven't been scheduled yet. Do you know anyone who knows Dr. Schuller?"

Almost everyone said, "No," but I kept it up. I stayed persistent. I was going to be on that show no matter what it took. Eventually, I found someone who worked for Bob Johnson (the owner of <u>Jet</u> and <u>Ebony</u> magazines at the time) and who knew Dr. Schuller. He asked if I was a public speaker, and I told him that I was. He asked if I was any good, and I said I was.

Well, the magazines needed a speaker, so I happily stepped up to help out. I did an amazing job ... so much so that Mr. Johnson himself asked me if there was anything he could do for me. I said, "I would love to be on the Dr. Robert Schuller Show."

He said, "I'll call Bob tomorrow."

When Dr. Schuller called me, I said, "This is not Dr. Robert Schuller."

He replied, "Yes, it is."

I said, "No way."

He said, "Yes, it is."

I got so nervous that I had to ask him to hold on while I went to use the bathroom!

Before I knew it, I was on his show, and millions of people saw me. It really helped to give me the boost that my career needed.

Persistence goes a long way. If you are persistent, you will find the right mentor. If you are persistent, you'll get through to them. Whether they want to mentor you or not is another thing, but with persistence, a "No" might eventually become a "Yes."

Don't stop trying at the first "No" - or even at the second one. Keep at it until you get what you want. Keep at it until you find the right mentor.

MENTORS THROUGH MEDIA

Can you have mentors who don't even know that they are mentoring you? Yes, believe it or not. You can.

Why would you want that?

Because some mentors are unavailable. Other mentors already have too many students. Some mentors may not even be alive anymore! This doesn't mean that you can't learn from them, though.

Using different forms of media, you are now able to access all kinds of different mentors without ever actually meeting them. In fact, you are doing it right now! You are reading this book, right now, which is giving you access to me, Les Brown.

Just like this book, you can read others by other great men and women. You can get insight into how they became successful, and you can use this insight to inspire greatness in your own life.

These days, you can actually take it a step further. There are many great mentors out there who record podcasts and share some of their greatest secrets for free! You can listen to these and soak up their knowledge any time.

Many of these greats are also on social media. You can follow them online, picking up valuable chunks of wisdom here and there. This medium also allows you to react to what they say, become part of the conversation in their community, and even reach out to them and ask them direct questions. Finally, different video formats, such as digital video downloads, DVDs, Blu Rays, and YouTube give you access to great mentors. You can see their passionate speeches given from the stage ... and you'll have the best seat in the house!

This reminds me. You are supposed to be reading 30 pages a day. What better pages to read than those written by someone you admire or emulate? Consider it an unofficial mentorship.

Read what the greats have to say, process this information, and implement it in your life. I guarantee that if you follow the advice they give you, whether you get it in written form, audio, or video, you'll get great results.

BEING IN THE LIGHT OF GREATNESS

The light of someone's greatness is illuminating, and you'll want to follow it. Eventually, your own light will begin to glow brighter, and others will want to follow you. From there, the cycle will continue, as you mentor others the way the greats mentored you.

Find someone who has what you want, and be persistent. If they agree to mentor you, listen to their advice and follow it. When the day comes that someone needs your help, be a mentor to them. Keep the cycle going, and allow others to grow and learn in the same way that you did.

Surround yourself with greatness and follow the advice of people at the top in your field. If you do, success is inevitable.

LAW 8:
LEAP AND GROW YOUR WINGS
ON THE WAY DOWN

This chapter has a simple message: to achieve greatness in your life, you should move before you are ready.

How does a small snowball become a giant one? As it rolls down the hill, it picks up more snow along with momentum. It grows and becomes larger, faster, and stronger. You are just like this snowball.

As you move toward your dreams, you'll notice that you pick up speed. You grow, you become powerful, and at a certain point, you become almost unstoppable.

The key to becoming a giant snowball is to allow the momentum in your life to push you forward, and to grow along the way. The trick is in getting started.

To build momentum, you need to get the ball rolling. A lot of people think this comes from careful planning. They plan every second of their day, every day of their week, every week of their month, every month of their year ... even every year of their life. All of this planning takes time. By the time they get going, today has passed, and it's tomorrow ... and that throws the schedule out of whack.

In order to build momentum, you need to get out of the planning phase. You need to **take action**.

This is the only way you'll accomplish anything.

It's been said that luck is where preparation meets opportunity. This is true, but there is such a thing as too much preparation. For many people, preparation is just an excuse not to act at all.

If you find yourself spending a lot of time in preparation for greatness, stop. You need to take the leap - and trust that on the way down, you'll figure out how to grow your wings.

When you look at my story and the stories of other successful people, you won't find a master plan that we carried out. Instead, you find desire, courage, and persistence.

For example, look at my story.

HOW I BECAME A MOTIVATIONAL SPEAKER

My beautiful mother, Mamie Brown, was an incredibly strong and brave woman. Although she didn't have much, she decided that she would take my brother and me in and give us all the love that she had. She didn't know how she was going to do it, but she was determined to make it work.

Was she 100% ready for the monumental task of raising us? Probably not. No one is ever truly ready to be a parent even equipped with lots of resources. However, because she wanted to care for us badly enough, there was no doubt she would find a way.

I grew up a bit of a troublemaker. I had a good heart, but I never did well in school and I made a lot of mistakes. Still, my mother believed in me, and so did my mentor Mr. Washington.

To be perfectly honest, he didn't believe in me at first. All he saw was a troublemaker with no direction. Through persistence, though, I made my drive and potential known to him, and he took me under his wing.

My mother and Leroy Washington helped me to see the greatness in me. My mother always believed that I was capable of greatness. All she wanted was to see me come into my own and achieve it. Both encouraged me to go for my dreams, even if I wasn't fully ready.

At first, I was dead set on being a disc jockey. I had always loved the idea of being an orator of some sort. My mother was a great storyteller, so I learned from the best!

Earlier in the book I told you the story of how with a little bit of persistence, I got the job at the radio station in Miami Beach. I was just getting coffee at first, but I still had an "in."

One day, a DJ got drunk on the job. I called the boss, who told me to find someone to fill in. I didn't even try. I called back and said no one could fill in. He told me to man the board, but to NOT get on the air. Of course, I went on the air.

And there it was. I was a radio DJ! It wasn't my dream career, but it was a step in that direction.

After a brief time in politics, I pursued a new career: motivational speaking. It combined my love for speaking and my love for helping others. It wasn't an easy road, though. I didn't simply make the decision to become a great speaker and suddenly fall into it.

At the same time, I didn't spend a lot of time making a detailed plan of steps to take. Instead, I looked for where opportunities seemed to be, and went in that direction.

At that time, the opportunity seemed to be in Detroit, where I knew some people who could help me achieve my dream. I found an office space and begged for rent for a few months. I got in trouble for sleeping in my office.

I didn't have any money, but I had passion. I was selling tapes that I made for ten dollars on the street, and I kept plugging away, working toward my dream of becoming a great public speaker and motivator. Before I knew it, I was making millions in speaking fees and videos. It didn't happen overnight, but I was persistent, and I didn't give up on my dreams.

Success began to build as I created momentum. Speaking gigs and networking led to bigger gigs, and eventually landed me on television. I still utilize that momentum today, and I still strive toward reaching and exceeding new goals.

In order to succeed, you need to take action. You need to make bold moves, even if you don't have everything planned out in advance. Going to the radio station day after day was a bold move. Jumping on the air when I was told not to was a bold move. Running for office was a bold move. Moving to Detroit, approaching heads of magazines, jumping on television … these were all bold moves made mostly with very little planning.

I built momentum, and I took action. That's what we are going to discuss for the rest of this chapter.

BUILDING MOMENTUM

With enough momentum, anything is possible. You can break through any barrier, and you can achieve the results that you are striving hard to achieve.

Look, I know it's easy to get sidetracked, and it's easy to get distracted. It's also easy to take a break, and allow yourself to believe that you can wait until later to work toward your dreams.

It's even easier to overthink, and to talk yourself out of achieving your dreams.

Remember, however, that your default mode is NOT working toward your dreams. You are used to thinking of your dreams as fiction. You limit them to your daydreaming mind, and you look at them as some grandiose desire that's fun to fantasize about, but never act on.

If you want to succeed, this has to change. You need to start seeing your dreams as very real and very achievable. You then need to work toward them with everything you've got, and to go at them full force.

There are no half measures with achieving your dreams. You either do it or you don't. You can work toward them and make progress, but ultimately you either achieve them - or you give up. There is no in between.

Now I want to discuss momentum in a few different ways. First, we'll talk about building momentum on a daily basis. I want you to wake up and immediately start building momentum in your life.

Next, I want to discuss momentum with regard to persistence. You need to keep plowing ahead, no matter what obstacles get in your way.

Finally, we'll discuss how to deal with the distractions that can get in the way of your momentum, slowing or even stalling your progress.

Momentum determines the size and speed of your growth, helping you succeed quicker and more efficiently.

DAILY MOMENTUM

Mornings

Start every morning by getting up immediately. Don't hit the "snooze" button on your alarm clock three times. Don't even hit it once! Jump out of bed in the morning, ready to face the day.

When your alarm goes off, I want you to immediately put your feet on the floor before anything else. When you gain consciousness, get up and make your bed. After that, sit on your freshly made bed (or get on your knees) and pray. Express gratitude for the gift of one more day on this beautiful planet, and ask for the strength to make it through the day.

If it helps you to get out of bed, put your alarm clock somewhere out of arm's reach. This will force you to physically get up to shut it off. Once you're up, you may as well stay up!

During your morning routine, do things to set a positive tone for the rest of your day. Get a little exercise in. Read 30 pages. Meditate. Journal. Do the exercises you've learned in this book.

Be sure to fill your body with nutrients. Take your time, cook something you like, and enjoy each bite. You may need to wake up a little earlier for this, but it's well worth it. It'll help you to eat less, and really take in what you are eating.

If you started every morning for the rest of your life like this, how many bad days will you really have?

Afternoons

It's no secret that most people hit a wall in the middle of the day. They get to two o'clock, and everything crashes from there. That's why when you are approaching this time of the day, you need to do something about it. You can't just give in to the crash; it will ruin your momentum for the rest of the day.

When you are coming up on that crash, take your lunch. Don't eat your lunch too early. Give yourself something to look forward to. When you eat your lunch, eat it slowly. This will help you avoid overeating. Many people overeat, and then get sluggish afterward. Instead, if you take your time, you'll know when you are full earlier and won't overeat.

Also, try to work some exercise into your midday routine. If you have a longer lunch hour, spend some of it moving around. Even a simple walk around the block makes an important statement about how much you care about your body. As long as you are moving, you'll reap the benefits of exercise and get the energy boost that you need to make it through the rest of the day.

Finally, truly step away. Don't work through your lunch, and don't spend your lunch worrying about work or checking work emails. Try to divorce yourself from your work, even if it's only for half an hour.

This will help you to recharge your batteries and mentally digest everything that you have taken in so far throughout the day. You'll be surprised at how much more efficient you are coming back with a clear head and a new set of eyes.

Evenings

Most people spend their entire evenings winding down, and that's okay. The problem is that they aren't constructive about how they do it. Instead of allowing themselves to process the day, they simply flop down on the couch and flip on mind-numbing TV until it's time to go to bed.

Then, as soon as their head hits the pillow, the band starts to play: "Why aren't I more successful? What am I doing with my life? How am I going to meet that deadline? Why didn't I check my emails earlier? Is my boss mad at me?"

Every thought that they were suppressing when they were zoned out in front of the tube kicks into high gear.

Sound familiar? If so, it's because you're approaching your evenings in the wrong way.

When you get home, take a moment to relax. You deserve it. Don't overdo it, though. You need to process your day and your feelings. Allow yourself to just **be**. This is a good time to journal and do the mindfulness exercises we talked about earlier. Some of your biggest breakthroughs will come from these periods of peace.

MOMENTUM AND PERSISTENCE

Persistence helps you to build momentum. When you keep pushing and striving for what you want, momentum builds. Persistence is one of the keys to building and maintaining momentum. It's what separates the winners from the losers.

If you hear "No" once, don't give up. Most successful people have been told "No" multiple times. Does that stop them from succeeding? Obviously not!

Did you know that The Beatles were turned down by a record label when they were first starting out? That's right, one of the most influential and famous bands of all time was told "No." Of course, that label's loss was another label's gain. Someone eventually said "Yes" and became very rich because of it.

You have something worthwhile to offer, don't give up. Don't take the first "No," or even the second. Don't let people without vision disrupt your progress. When you hit hurdles, and when you get turned down, you need to maintain your momentum.

You have to persist until you get the answer you want, and you can't stop there! Even when you reach your goals, you need to keep moving forward. I guarantee you that when you hit your goal, more goals will pop up. There's always more success, and there are always new challenges.

Once you get into the habit of being persistent, you'll see that accomplishing your current goals and accomplishing new goals can be easier than ever.

DISTRACTIONS TO MOMENTUM

No matter how persistent you are, there will always be distractions that get in between you and your goal. These distractions may temporarily pull you away from reaching your goal, and they can even stop you if you let them.

Here is how to deal with some of these distractions.

Fear and the Need for Safety

One of the biggest distractions that people run into is fear of economic insecurity. They fear that their safe, normal life will be threatened or disappear. In a way, it will. When you decide to go full force and jump into achieving your goals, you have to take risks.

Be prepared for this, but don't let it scare you or slow you down. Instead, defeat your fear of the unknown with knowledge. If you know what to expect going in, you won't be as worried about the bumps that you hit in the road.

Remember, you aren't taking the safe path to victory. Be prepared for ups and downs on your way to greatness.

Laziness

Many people are so used to lazily coasting by that when the time comes to really make a push, they either don't know how or they sit around and hope it happens magically. To make changes and maintain momentum, you need to be putting in the work.

Keep your eye on the prize, and do not allow sloth to be your downfall. Get in the habit of working hard, and always do a little more than you need to do. Train yourself to respond to challenges by rising up to the occasion instead of avoiding them.

Other People

Sometimes people will stand in the middle of your path and try to flag you down. Their arms will wave for you to stop. When you do, all they have to say is that the road ahead is dangerous and that you should take a safer path.

DON'T slow down for these people. Just because they want to take a safer path in life doesn't mean you do. While still respecting them, drive around them, and keep making your way toward your goals.

STOP OVERTHINKING

While it's important to have an idea of where you're going, many people use planning as way to delay or altogether avoid taking action. They throw themselves into imaginary scenarios, and try to think through every possible step of their journey.

In reality, life is unpredictable. There will be problems that arise, and you simply cannot plan for them. Don't spend your entire life drawing up plans.

From a Robert Burns poem:

"The best laid schemes of mice and men go often askew."

You may have heard something similar, like

"The best laid plans of mice and men often go awry."

The point is that no matter how great your plans are, they can and often do go off course. Life doesn't always go the way you want it to go, or the way you plan for it to go. Because of this, you need to learn how to jump in feet first.

JUMP IN FEET FIRST

When I wanted to become a motivational speaker, I moved to Detroit with almost no idea how I would do it. I got an office with barely any money, and I often slept on the floor. Obviously, I hadn't planned very far ahead! Still, this lit a fire under me.

I knew that I had to succeed. I had no other option. I put my back against the wall, and I had to battle my way out.

In order to really get the best out of yourself, you need to jump in feet first. You need to give it your all, even if you don't always know the next steps. You'll find that the path begins to reveal itself.

You'll see new opportunities open up where you never expected them, and you'll see a divine light that shows you the way. Listen to this light. If you second-guess it, or let something lead you astray, you may have trouble finding your path again.

ADJUST YOUR COURSE AS YOU GO

Life doesn't have a compass that shows you the way. If you find some sort of a compass, know that it's compromised. It won't always show you the right path.

Instead, trust your gut, and adjust your course as you go.

There have been many times that I thought I was making progress toward reaching a goal, but the path that I thought would lead me to victory took a sharp turn. I had to adjust, and I had to make new plans on the spot.

Over time, though, an instinct kicked in. I learned to make quick adjustments without a lot of fear and rumination. I learned to roll with the punches and adjust my strategy for success.

YOUR WINGS WILL SPROUT

When it's time to make the big leap, trust that your wings will sprout. Consider a bird's first flight. The bird doesn't know exactly what it's doing, and it could very well plummet to the earth. Still, it jumps from the branch and its wings open. It takes flight and feels the freedom.

You need to take that leap. You have to trust that your wings can carry you, and you need to trust the instincts that you were born with to take flight. Birds don't sit around planning how they're going to fly. They leap. They adjust as the wind rustles their feathers, and they know that it's do or die. You either fly and adjust, or you hit the ground. That might sound scary, but most of the time hitting the ground isn't that painful, and you can quickly get back up.

Most of the time though, your wings will sprout and you'll surprise yourself with how high you'll soar.

MOMENTUM AND TAKING THE LEAP

In this chapter, we discussed gaining momentum and avoiding distractions. We also discussed how a lack of planning can actually be a powerful tool for success, and how sometimes you simply need to take a leap of faith and learn to fly on the way down.

I'm not encouraging you to jump from the branch while I sit, safe and sound on the bough of the tree. I've jumped from the branch. I've leaped, and sometimes I didn't have the best landing. Over time, though, I learned how to soar. I learned how to pick up momentum, and I learned how to fly even higher.

You can do this. If you do, you will spread your wings and soar to new heights.

LAW 9:
CREATE MULTIPLE STREAMS OF INCOME

One of the most common questions I get is how to create wealth and financial freedom. Applying what you've learned so far in this book will take you a long way. To get all the way there, you need to apply one simple strategy that all wealthy people share: multiple streams of income.

This strategy is one of the best things you can do to create wealth and financial freedom in your life.

This might sound crazy and hard, but it's actually a lot easier than you'd think. It's also a lot smarter. While you may have one job and you feel secure in it, job security is rarely guaranteed. Because your income is tied directly to your time, your income potential is limited.

What happens to you if your company goes out of business or gets sold? What if the company decides to downsize? What happens if they decide that someone else is more qualified? Or what if your boss simply doesn't like you?

You could easily find yourself without a job ... with no money coming in.

The traditional 20th century way of living is to make money at one job for the rest of your working life. You might change companies here and there. You may even make a huge life decision to change your career.

But no matter what you're doing, it only involves one job. If you are desperate, you may pick up a part-time job for extra money, but it isn't supposed to be long-term.

The idea of having one job as your only source of income, however, has become old fashioned. For many different reasons, people don't stay at one job or one company as long as they used to, and companies no longer invest in their employees the way they used to. This has led to the notion that people are expendable, and that means that your "one job" is always hanging in the balance.

I want you to think about someone (it could be you) who had one great job. That job was everything they ever wanted. Maybe they went to college for many years to earn a degree that would help land them an internship. Maybe they got their foot in the door at their dream company, and spent years working their way up the ladder. They never thought of doing anything else. Their spouse didn't work, and they built a life around this one paycheck.

Then, one day, they got called into the office. They were told that the company couldn't afford to keep the whole department.

They got the ax.

They had some savings, but that only lasted so long. Searching for a new job, especially at the high position they'd reached, took months, even years! They might eventually settle for a job at a far lower status and income, just to keep up with the bills.

This is a terrifying situation. Sadly, a lot of people I've known have found themselves in this position. You may have found yourself in it as well.

You may even be experiencing it right now!

While you can't change the past, you can make changes for the future and learn from your mistakes.

If having one job isn't the best approach, what are you supposed to do? How are you supposed to build an additional layer of security? And how do you find the time?

There is a way to make money that doesn't rely on only one source of income.

MULTIPLE STREAMS OF INCOME

The idea of having multiple streams of income has been around for a while. The wealthy have been doing it since the beginning of civilization. For many, setting up multiple streams of income is how they got wealthy.

You can utilize multiple streams of income to build and maintain your own wealth. Having multiple streams of income also helps to increase your security; if one stream of income fails, you have others to fall back on. You can set it up so that the streams are equal, or you can simply have some backups to get you by. Either way, having several will help to keep you afloat if one stream fails.

PASSIVE INCOME

Having multiple streams of income doesn't mean having multiple full time jobs. It means having as many sources of passive income as possible.

Passive income helps you break the connection between time and income. Here's what I mean:

Right now, if you work a typical job, you get paid based on the number of hours you work. The problem is that there's a limit to the number of hours in each day. A limited number of hours per day means a limited amount of money per day.

I make a substantial amount of money from speaking engagements, but even if I stopped speaking tomorrow, I would still have money coming in from residuals and investments I've made. You can replicate that in your own life.

There are a variety of different forms of income that you can create, and with each new stream, your wealth will grow. You probably won't be able to start them all at once. It'll take time. For some reason, that's one of the biggest objections I hear from people about setting up multiple income streams: It's virtually impossible to launch them all at once.

That's why I want you to focus on building one at a time, but to always be building. You should always be adding new streams of income, or building on the ones that you already have.

I read an article recently about a woman who created about a dozen different streams of income. She had them all running simultaneously! It was brilliant. She looked at every aspect of her life and found a way to monetize each one. She also invested in real estate and other opportunities, allowing her to earn even more.

Sure, there was a lot of juggling going on, but her setup allowed her the flexibility to turn her income streams on or off, like a faucet. She was able to have a couple running, a few running, or all of them running at once!

While you don't need to build twelve sources of income, it's smart to have a few. You can start by building around the assets that you already have. From there, you can move into investing and growing additional assets.

STACKING YOUR ASSETS

Before I walk you through the different streams of income that you can set up to build your wealth, we need to discuss **stacking assets**.

You see, a lot of people want to jump into being self-reliant and making a bunch of money all at once. That's fantastic, but sometimes you simply don't have all of the assets that you will ultimately need.

For example, we don't all have a lot of cash lying around. That's okay for now. You can start by creating income from the assets you do have. Once you've saved enough money, you can start investing in other forms of income to build your own steady stream.

The good news is that even if you have debt, bills and responsibilities, there are probably assets you can invest in right now. They don't require a big investment either. You can set them up with what you already have, or with less than $100.

I want to remind you that you only go around once. No matter what challenges you face, no matter how hard it gets, consider the fact that when you are on your deathbed, you'll have to look back and see the kind of life that you CHOSE to live.

Most people's biggest regrets are that they didn't take more risks, and that they didn't follow their dreams. It's rare that you hear someone on their deathbed say, "Wow, I sure am glad I took the safe road!"

That's why I want you to take "can't" out of your vocabulary.

Go ahead: Say that this will be hard. Say that it will take time. Say that it will take true grit. Say whatever you want; just don't say that you can't.

Can't is one of the biggest lies that we are fed. It's used to keep us in line and to keep the people who are on top in control.

You see, many people have a vested interest in your failure. If you succeed, you become the competition. They don't want you taking a piece of their pie. So they try to sell you on your inability to succeed.

They sell your loved ones the same idea, and they train them to spread the message of **can't**. YOU are responsible for breaking this cycle. YOU are responsible for spreading the gospel of **CAN**.

I want you to say to yourself "**I CAN**."

Say it with conviction. Believe it!

I CAN.

I want you to spread the gospel of I CAN, and I want you to live it in your everyday life.

Think about this. I'll remind you again later, because it's extremely important. You need to know that when you start becoming independently wealthy, that it IS possible. You need to BELIEVE in wealth, and you need to adopt a wealth mindset.

Now, let's get back to stacking because it's how you're going start your wealthy I CAN life.

As I outline the different ways that you can build wealth and create multiple streams of income, I am going to start with the most immediate ones. These are your start-off points, because they utilize resources that you already have and can monetize, or they only require a very small fee.

Next, I will get into intermediate level streams that will help you grow your wealth enough to make bigger investments. Finally, we'll talk about the bigger investments that cost a bit more but last as long as you like.

Choose at least one of the following income stream ideas to get yourself going. If you already have a steady income, you don't have to give it up. Just start one of these on the side to start building your stack.

Over time, transition to more passive forms of income. Remember, to become truly wealthy, you must break that connection between time and income.

FREELANCING

If you have a skill, you can sell your services as a freelancer, in addition to work that you're already doing. While initially you will get paid based on the time you put in, over time you can create a stream of passive income by getting clients and outsourcing the hourly work to other freelancers for less than you charge.

There are all kinds of freelancing opportunities. If you feel that you have a good grasp on the English language, or if you think that you have a knack for writing, freelance writing and editing is a good place to start. There is always a need for strong writers and editors.

If you have a keen eye and a knack for art and design, graphic design may be the perfect way for you to make money online. This takes quite a bit of skill, but if you can become a proficient graphic designer, you can make quite a bit of money from your own home! Graphic design is in high demand, and you can specialize in anything from web design to brochures, book covers, magazine covers, and more.

Has anyone ever told you that you have a great voice? Are you a natural orator and a great story teller? If so, freelance voice over work may be the perfect field for you. As a voice over artist, you can get paid to narrate books, do voice recordings for different forms of media, advertising agencies, and more.

Voice artistry takes a little practice, and if you want to have the best quality recordings possible, you'll need the right equipment. Sure, you can get started with cheap or free equipment and a lower-end microphone, but if you want the higher paying jobs, you might opt to spend a few extra dollars on professional equipment.

Other freelancing opportunities include consulting, data entry, photography, and entertainment. Just think about the problems companies have, and which of those problems you can solve. Tap into your network and go to websites and events specifically designed to connect freelancers with employers.

It's easier than ever to get side work, so take advantage of those opportunities!

CRAFTS

Creating custom crafts is affordable, and if you are talented, it can be pretty easy. The great thing about craft projects is how varied they are. You can create jewelry, t-shirts, hats ... whatever your heart desires!

Even though the cost of supplies can add up, selling your crafts is cheap or even free. Websites like Etsy.com allow you to set up your own store to sell your crafts online, or you can sell the old fashioned way, at fairs, or on the street.

Some crafts (purse making, for instance) take great skill. Others (T-shirt printing) are more simple. Go with what you are good at and what you enjoy doing. Once you get good at it, you'll build a reputation and your popularity will spread. If you come up with a truly unique idea or design, you could even corner the market and start making some real money!

THE GIG ECONOMY

With new apps, it is easier than ever to bring in extra income during your free time. You can get paid to drive, perform tasks, deliver groceries, walk dogs, and even rent out a spare bedroom.

While these are great opportunities to bring in some extra income, they are somewhat limited because your income is still directly connected to your time. However, the extra income you make from gigs can help you quickly pay down debt or even make savvy investments that you can build on later.

ONLINE BUSINESSES

We live in amazing times. With the right system, you can build an online business that can support you and your family for a small upfront investment compared to other types of businesses.

People have made millions of dollars starting internet marketing companies. Once these are off the ground and running, they can be pretty low maintenance. This allows you to diversify and expand your business.

Make sure you take your time to learn about different systems for online businesses. Some of the best include digital publishing, affiliate marketing, blogging, selling apps, and running an ecommerce store. If you treat it seriously, like a business and not as a get rich quick scheme, you can succeed with any of these business models.

SPEAKING

This one is near and dear to my heart for obvious reasons. Anyone, and I mean anyone, can succeed as a speaker with enough practice and grit. You have the power to impact people's lives with your words, and it would be a shame if you didn't use that power.

How do you get better at speaking? You just do it. There are all kinds of groups dedicated to helping you become a better speaker. Toastmasters is the largest of these groups.

How do you get speaking gigs? First, know your audience. Instead of speaking to a general audience, get specific. Which group can you offer the most value to? Which group will benefit most from your stories, experiences and wisdom?

You might need to start by speaking for free, but once you start making connections and build up a solid portfolio of speeches, you will be able to get paid well to speak. Like any other opportunity in this chapter, you just need the right system and persistence.

INVESTING

You don't have to be Warren Buffett to become a successful investor. In fact, most good investing is based in common sense. Two of the best places to invest are real estate and the stock market.

With real estate, as long as the property doesn't somehow become devalued, the value should go up over time. Sure, there may be hits to the economy here and there. Don't buy at the peak of a real estate bubble (when prices are higher than actual values), and think long-term and you will generally see a nice return on your investment over time. More important, you'll have tenants paying your mortgage and property taxes through their rent, which means you're building equity at no cost to yourself.

Stocks carry a higher risk. Meet with an experienced financial planner and choose a mix of low and high risk stocks, and you can create an impressive money making portfolio. Investing in stocks is something that you should do with extra money, though. Don't tie up all of your funds in the stock market.

STARTING A PHYSICAL BUSINESS

Most of the opportunities we've covered above can be turned into full businesses with relatively small startup costs and little financial risk. With a physical business, however, you need a physical location and you need supplies. This makes it high risk, and it will likely take a lot of time to get your business up and running.

Still, starting your own brick and mortar business can be extremely rewarding, and allows you to serve people in person. It also allows you to focus on whatever you want: A clothing store, a restaurant ... you decide!

If you don't want to build a business from scratch, you can always buy an existing business and make the changes it needs to become more profitable.

If One Fails...

If you have multiple streams of income and one fails, you have the security of being able to rely on the others. Multiple streams of income also let you build wealth instead of just making money to live and pay bills. You can start making enough to invest, and put into savings and your retirement.

Don't get tied to one job that could be taken away at any moment. Keep yourself protected and create your own wealth with multiple streams of income.

LAW 10:
LIGHT UP EACH ROOM YOU ENTER

Throughout this book, we have discussed how to create success and turn your dreams into reality. While this is important, it is only one side of the coin.

A lot of people become successful, but can't hold on to their success. While there are a few different reasons for this, one of the biggest is that they lose track of their sense of fulfillment; they stop enjoying the process.

They get so wrapped up in making money that they forget that there are much more important aspects of success.

You see, people define success in different ways. To some, success is starting a successful business. To others, success is raising respectable and loving children. No matter how you define success, you need to make sure that you do what is important to you, and that you enjoy the process.

I've spoken with people whose goal is to make money. While money is a great byproduct of success, it is not a sustainable goal. When all you see are dollar signs, you lose track of your happiness and your sense of self. Your goal shouldn't be simply to make money. If you apply what you learn in this book, the money will come, but that shouldn't be your focus.

Focus instead on building a life of fulfillment. You should be excited to start each and every day, and this excitement comes from loving what you do. If you can get to this point, you'll find yourself enjoying the process. It won't just be about being successful anymore; it will be about doing something you love which also happens to build your wealth.

Let's say that you want to become a concert pianist. (If you've never played an instrument in your life, this is a pretty long-term goal. Don't get me wrong; it's very possible. I once met a woman in her nineties who played piano beautifully - and she hadn't started until she was in her sixties.)

Anyway, let's say you want to be a pianist. You can't focus on the money up front. That will only get you so far. Even if you practice every day for hours on end, it will still take years to get to the point where you can be a professional concert pianist.

During the time that you are learning to play, you won't make any money playing piano. At a certain point, you'll realize that the only way to keep going will be to enjoy the process.

If you don't enjoy practicing the piano, jamming out, and learning music theory, you'll never make it. That's not to say that every second will be fun. You may get bored running the same scales over and over. When the time comes to utilize those scales, though, you'll know them like the back of your hand.

Eventually, you'll see opportunities opening up. Maybe you'll join a jazz band and make some money on the weekend. Maybe you'll teach, building your skills while passing on your knowledge and making money. All of this time, you may be trying out for different gigs until finally, the right person hears you play. Suddenly, you are on stage, playing the piano for hundreds or even thousands of people.

All of this started with one note. Then, another note. A chord here, a scale there. Years of practice … and then you start making money.

This is only possible if playing the piano leaves you feeling fulfilled. You should feel a deep hunger - a desire to learn all you can - that consumes you. You may actually lose money by paying for equipment and lessons, but that's okay, because it is all part of the process, and you LOVE the process.

If, after a while, no matter how hard you try, you can't enjoy it, you may want to quit. Maybe this is not for you. Don't quit right away, don't quit just because it gets hard. Quit if you realize that you have no passion for it, and that you are only doing something for the paycheck.

The next few chapters are going to shift from building success to creating value. If you do the right thing and take the next steps, you'll find that you can not only create value in your own life, but also in the lives of the people around you.

You'll become a beacon of hope. People will see you as an example of someone who has no quit in them. They'll think of you - and they'll smile. "That's the guy who's always happy," they'll think. "I want to be like him."

This isn't about building admiration. It's about being the kind of person who is admirable. It's about living a respectable life whose byproduct is respect from others. When you are living in line with the right values, and you trying your absolute best to do the right thing and help others on their path, you'll find that your life becomes richer.

Not only will new opportunities manifest, but you will find that life is just easier. Speaking with people, building your business, finding a romantic partner ... all of it will seem so much easier. That's because you will be on the path that was chosen for you.

God has a plan, and if you stick to it and don't get in the way of others achieving their happiness, you'll find a deep joy. Will there still be tough times? Of course. But you'll have your eye on the prize, and you'll have a song in your heart.

In this chapter, we're going to discuss your relationship with value Consider this essential question: Are you a **value giver** or a **value taker**?

VALUE GIVER OR TAKER

We are all both value givers and value takers. That's just the nature of the universe. If you give everything away without taking, you'll starve! If you take everything without giving, no one will be around you because you're a mooch.

There is a fine balance between being a giver and a taker, and it is built around symbiosis. All of your relationships should be symbiotic in nature, in which both parties receive an acceptable balance. Of course, not all relationships will be equal. For instance, you will never fully pay back your parents for raising you. That's okay. You can pay them back by treating them with love and respect, and helping them in their later years.

I want to discuss who you are taking from and why. Then I want to discuss who you are giving to, and how to give more efficiently. The goal here is perspective. You want to better understand your relationships, and you want to make sure that these relationships are in balance.

Let's start with how you are receiving, and from whom.

How You Receive Value

While we are all value takers, a positive relationship should involve **receiving** value which you are freely given and which you accept with grace and gratitude.

I want you to take an inventory of the value that you are receiving: Write out a list of the people from who you have received value, now and in the past. This list could include a sibling, parent, friend, mentor ... anyone who has given you something without expecting anything directly in return. Consider the relationships where you were given something out of love and care.

Once you have these relationships listed out, write down how you received each person's gifts, and what you did to reciprocate. These don't have to be perfectly equal exchanges. For instance, you were raised by your parents, and in return you may have thanked them as an adult and done everything you could to help them out as they aged.

Once you write all of this out, you'll get a better idea of the nature of the relationship that you have with others. It'll be tough, but I'm going to ask you to be brutally honest. I want you to really think about how you receive and whether you are more of a taker than a receiver.

If you find that you take more than you receive, you need to make some fundamental changes in the way that you interact with others. The nature of your relationships is unbalanced, and in order to be the best person you can be, you need to adjust these interactions.

The first step is awareness. Simply being aware of how you respond to people's kindness will help you to start making changes.

Next, consider how you can do better in the future. How can you change the way that you receive incoming gifts so you are no longer taking without giving value?

At times, being thankful and helping out when the gift giver is in need may be enough. Other times you may be able to give back directly, with money, flowers, buying them dinner, or whatever else is appropriate. Don't try to force a gift on anyone, though. Sometimes people do nice things simply for the happiness of others. (You should be doing that too, and we'll get to that in a few minutes.)

Finally, I want you to look at the people from whom you have taken value and think about how you can set this right. This is especially important for people that you have repeatedly taken value from, like a close friend, family member, or spouse.

I want you to speak with these people, and let them know that you realize that you were given a gift without appropriately reciprocating. Then, consider a thoughtful way you can offer to pay them back. The key word there is "offer." They may not want anything in return other than your acknowledgement that they helped you, and your thanks.

Once you've gotten all of this in order, you can begin to change the way that you receive and better appreciate the gifts that you are given.

HOW TO GIVE VALUE

Let's discuss how you can actively give value. It's important to keep in mind that just because you are willing to give, you shouldn't always expect anything in return. Yes, there will be times that you create value and rightfully expect something, like when you work for a paycheck. But other times you can and should give value simply because it's the right thing to do.

In order to enrich your life and the lives of people around you, you should do things for other people simply to put good out into the world. These could be acts as small as holding the door open for somebody or as large as adopting a child, like my mother did for me. These are ways that you can put good energy into the world, and surround yourself with positivity.

Doing good for others will also help you to put things into perspective. When you volunteer at a homeless shelter, for instance, you start to learn about the people who are there and their stories. When you begin to see that they aren't very different from you, you grow a new level of compassion for your fellow man.

I want you to think about some good deeds that you can work into your life, and some ways that you can help others. When you think about this, don't think about how this will benefit you. Instead, think about the joy and happiness that you can bring to someone's life.

This could fundamentally change the way you see and do things. You'll become more conscious of the people around you, and you'll want to make decisions that help to better not only your life, but other's lives.

I don't write books and give speeches simply to make a profit. I already have plenty of money. I genuinely enjoy helping other people to see their potential. I want other people to be happy, and I want them to discover the life that they were meant to live.

Honestly, if my life as a public speaker hadn't panned out, I'd still be out there trying to make a difference in the world. I have been given many gifts, and it gives me genuine joy to share them with others.

Start thinking about who you give to and why. Do you only give your time and energy to make money or to get something you want? Or do you take time out of your life to help others improve theirs?

Trust me. There is enough time to both make money and to help others. The question is whether or not you are spending your extra time helping others or simply yourself.

BRING OUT GREATNESS IN OTHERS

One of the greatest gifts you can give to someone else is to help them unlock greatness within them. That might sound like a lot, but it really isn't.

When I was young, I was diagnosed with a learning disability. According to my school administrators, I would never be able to learn like the other kids. Because that's what I was told, it was what I believed.

Then one day I was in class and a teacher said, "Young man, go to the board and work this problem out for me." I said, "Well, sir, I can't do that." He said, "Why not?" I said, "I'm not one of your students." He said, "Look at me." "Yes, sir." "Go to the board and work the problem out anyhow." I said, "I can't, sir."

The other students started laughing. They said, "He's Leslie. He's got a twin brother, Wesley. Wesley is smart. Leslie is his DT." The teacher asked, "What's DT?" "He's the dumb twin." The teacher looks at me and I said "I am, sir."

As the students laughed, the teacher came from behind his desk and looked at me. He said, "Don't you ever say that again. Someone's opinion of you does not have to become your reality." That was a turning point in my life.

On one hand, I was humiliated, but on the other hand, I was liberated, because with that one statement, this myth that I could never achieve what my fellow students could was shattered. All sorts of possibilities opened up before me. Without that one individual giving me a taste of my potential, I wouldn't have had the mental strength to build the life that I've built.

Be that person for others. Show them that they too can be great, as long as they don't underestimate their own potential.

BEING A BEACON

Have you ever met someone who could magically brighten up your day? Maybe it was your grandmother, a school teacher, or simply a friendly face at your local coffee shop. That person just seemed to make everything better. They smiled at you, and spoke to you in a voice that told you on a deeper level that they cared and that things would be all right.

These people are beacons of hope. In a wild storm, they are the light in the lighthouse that guides you home. These are some of the most valuable people on earth because they spread love simply by existing. When they interact with other people, their primary focus is brightening the other person's day, listening to what they have to say, and being there for support when it seems like no one else is around.

The thing is, being a beacon isn't a super power. We all have it in us. We all have the ability to make other people's lives brighter, and to be the person that others flock to when the night seems darkest.

Most people just haven't discovered it in themselves yet. They haven't seen the light that they possess which can guide others through the darkness. This is usually because they are so involved with themselves that they never learn how to shine for others.

In fact, most people don't ever think about being a beacon. They may notice and even cherish the beacons in their lives, but they simply don't see themselves in this way.

Well, I want to tell you that YOU can - and should - be a beacon.

Be there for others, not because it will help you get ahead, but because it will help them find peace and joy. In return, you'll have the knowledge that you made someone else's life better. This is an invaluable gift. You can go to bed knowing that you put good out into the world. When things seem dark, you can lighten them up by thinking about the smile you put on someone's face.

Being a beacon is something that you should strive toward until it becomes effortless, until being kind and loving is your default mode. People will want to be around you, because when they are, they will feel as if the world is a bit brighter.

One of the most valuable things that you can give others is **hope**. Here's how you can start to become a beacon.

BRIGHTENING OTHER PEOPLE'S DAYS

"When you're smiling, the world smiles with you."

This is the name of a famous Louis Armstrong song, and I believe it's a truly inspirational quote as well. It sums up everything we are talking about in a beautiful way. Your smile and your ability to brighten up the world around you are very powerful. You'll find that when you are upbeat, the people around you are upbeat as well. You can cheer people up, and you can help them to live more positive lives.

Make it a goal of yours to brighten other people's days just a little bit. Whether it's with a smile, a gesture, or a helping hand, you should always be focusing on how to improve the quality of someone else's life. Not only will it make their day better, but it will make your day better ... and it will make the universe a better place.

Try to focus on other people and their needs. See what you can do to help them to achieve their goals, and make yourself available. You never know; they may return this kindness when you need it most.

REMEMBER NAMES AND CONVERSATIONS

Another great - and simple - way to make someone's day brighter is to remember their name and the conversation you last had with them. I heard someone speaking about how Tom Cruise does this. He takes the time to get to know everyone on the set, and he remembers their name and the last conversation he had with them. He'll walk up to people and say things like, "Hey Chris! Great to see you. How's your wife? Did she get the promotion?"

Something as small as remembering a relative stranger's name and showing that you were listening to what they had to say can dramatically improve their lives. They know that someone was listening, and more important, that someone cares.

This is something you should practice starting NOW. Come up with a pneumonic way for remembering names if you need to. If you still have trouble, keep a journal of names and conversations. Obviously, don't take notes while you are speaking with them, but take a moment when you have a private moment to write their name and what you spoke about.

After a while, remembering people and making them feel special will become a habit.

BEING A BEACON IS A CHOICE

You choose whether or not you want to be a beacon in other people's lives. You can shine brightly, or you can fade away into the night. I'll tell you what, though. You'll feel a lot better if you spend your time helping others and making them feel better.

Say nice things. Smile more. Remember people. Then watch both their quality of life and yours grow.

ATTRACTION OVER EGO

The last thing I want to discuss is how you can better attract people into your life AND achieve your goals: By letting go of your ego.

Have you ever met someone who tries too hard? You can spot their neediness from a mile away! People don't want to be around other people who always want something, or people who talk about themselves all the time.

In order to succeed in life, you need to attract people with love and support, rather than bravado. As they get to know you, they'll recognize your greatness. There is no need to endlessly promote yourself.

Let's break this down a little further.

YOU VERSUS YOUR ACCOMPLISHMENTS

Everyone knows people who brag. All they ever seem to want to talk about is their accomplishments. They want the world to know their greatness, and they need to be seen as great immediately. These people are insecure, and they have taken any success that they have amassed and turned it into something ugly.

No one likes a bragger. Bragging is the absolute worst way to try to attract people into your life. Your inflated ego is like a giant sign that tells people that you are insecure, and they'll steer clear of you. You will miss out on a lot of opportunities not only for business, but to meet and connect with special people.

All of the people that I know who have accomplished great things and are happy have a certain vibe about them. They are incredibly approachable, and they steer the conversation in a way that makes YOU feel more powerful. When you walk away, you're thinking more about how they made you feel than who they are in their respective industry.

Have you ever met someone famous? I bet if you have, they left a pretty strong impression on you. Either you tell your friends how rude they were, or you tell them how nice and positive they were. Everyone has bad moments, but usually you can tell who is trying to make a positive difference in the world and who isn't.

There is a lot more power in the way that you make people feel than in your accomplishments. I want to repeat this, because it's important:

There is a lot more power in the way that you make people feel than in your accomplishments.

You remember great people because of the way they make you feel. They may impart great wisdom upon you. You may or may not remember it. But you WILL remember how they made you feel. You'll remember that they made you feel powerful, and that they stripped away your self-doubt with their positivity and kindness.

A GOOD ATTITUDE WILL PUSH YOU FURTHER

Whether it is in business, in your love life, or in your personal life, a good attitude will push you further than you ever thought that you could go. That's because people want to help you when you have a good attitude. They will want to contribute to your life because they believe in the love that you share. They will see a good person who is trying to reach their dreams, and it will remind them that there is goodness in the world, and there is hope.

Be this beacon of hope for people, and strive every day to make the people that you meet feel special, worthy, and loved.

BE A GIVER

In this chapter, we've discussed being a giver and a taker. While you will always be both, try as hard as you can to contribute more to the lives of others than you take. Not only will you feel better, but you'll leave the world a better place. You'll also see that your business opportunities grow, and the people you surround yourself with will reflect your values. Positivity attracts positivity.

Be a beacon of hope, and always be looking for ways to put a smile on people's faces even if it just means remembering their name and a few things about them. Every little bit helps, and even a small gesture could turn their whole day around.

Enjoy the people around you, enjoy the process, and spread the happiness and love that you want in your life.

LAW 11:
LEAD BY SERVING THE NEEDS OF OTHERS

Everything you do should make the world a better place. Every action should be motivated by a desire to leave the world better than you found it. Your goal should be to help yourself by helping other people.

I know all this may sound different from most books about how to attain success. Most businesspeople will tell you the opposite. They will tell you that success is all about getting yours, regardless of what happens to other people.

While you may succeed financially that way, you'll soon find that your success is hollow. You won't lie comfortably in bed, and when you get older, you'll see your remaining relationships deteriorate. No one will want to be around your negative and destructive energy. The only people who will stick around are those looking to benefit from your success. If this success diminishes, those people will disappear.

As you're building your dream life, it is crucially important that it helps others too. If you create a product, you should believe in it! You should never put out a product that you would not buy. Everything you do should be done with integrity; otherwise you'll never see your success grow.

Have you ever ordered pizza from a pizza place that doesn't care about the quality of their food? Have you gone to a corner store that is not swept and the person behind the counter looks at you like you are a waste of his or her time? Did you want do business with these people again? I bet not.

Sometimes these business owners get lucky. Sometimes they'll corner the market in an area without competition. When the competition comes, though, they quickly go under. If they try to expand, their expansion fails. This is because that level of service won't fly under every circumstance.

You've probably also experienced a new store or a restaurant that instantly embeds itself in the community as soon as it opens. These businesses are good neighbors. They treat their customers well and they sell high quality products or services. The owners run their business with integrity not only because it helps with sales, but because it's the right thing to do. They started their business because they had a dream and a love for what they do, instead of only trying to make a quick buck.

When it's time to follow your dreams, set your goals, and build the life that you've always wanted, you need to consider how you can do these things while being serving the people around you. This includes your customers, family, community, and more.

You should be able to look yourself in the mirror every morning and see a good person who means well. If you are ashamed to look yourself or others in the eye, you aren't doing it right!

In the previous chapter, we discussed how you can brighten people's days with your positive energy. In this chapter, we are going to talk about brightening people's lives by providing the best value you possibly can, and how this will also help YOU to achieve YOUR goals. You'll learn about how the creation of value can lead to a better life for everyone, including you.

Let's start this discussion with how you can be of service to others. Then we'll discuss how service can lead to personal fulfillment. Finally we'll go over the different service opportunities that you can take advantage of starting today.

BE OF SERVICE

When most people hear the word "service," they cringe. The term may elicit thoughts of serving tables, long-gone societies where people served the royals, working customer service, or another manner of service position.

The word "service" has been tainted, and that's a real shame. The reality is that service is a beautiful thing, and when you are serving your community, and your fellow human beings.

I want to discuss being of service with you because I know that it will enhance your life. You'll succeed in your field, but you'll also become a pillar of your community. People will love to be around you, and because of this, they will support you with all of their heart.

You Should ALWAYS Be Serving the Needs of Others

Service isn't something that you only do once a week and then forget about it. You don't get "service bucks" that you can save up and spend on building your life. Service is an ongoing thing, and you should take the service opportunities that are presented to you. God would not put someone in need in your path if you weren't meant to be of service.

Here's a caveat: You may choose not to serve people who refuse to serve themselves. Service is about helping to boost someone up, not doing things for them. You don't want to become an enabler, but you DO want to help when you can. There is a fine line that may take a while to learn, but over time you'll get a feel for who really wants a boost and who just wants a handout.

For those who do reach out for help, help them. Spend a little of your off-time helping others. If you see someone who needs help, offer to help them. If they decline, that's fine. Leave them be. The important thing is that you offer, and that you mean it. If the time comes that they do want help, they know who to call.

I am a big advocate of answering the phone for people I know. If I can't, I try to get back to them as soon as possible. You never know when people are in need. The phone call may be a casual, "Hello," but it also may be someone reaching out because they need you. Don't miss that call.

Serving others will also help you to get out of your own head. Suddenly, your fears and anxieties will start to slip away. Your life will be put into clear perspective as you see the people around you struggling just as you are. If you're a parent, you know EXACTLY what I am talking about!

After a while, your instinct to help will kick in and take precedence over your selfish need to complain. You'll learn to simply listen when someone needs to vent, and you'll learn how to help when help is requested.

You should always take opportunities to help others. You will even want to seek some opportunities to help, and to give direct help where it is needed.

DIFFERENT TYPES OF SERVICE

We are going to go into detail about different service positions later in this chapter, but I want to briefly mention what service entails. You can serve in a variety of different ways, including:

- Giving advice
- Volunteering
- Coaching
- Feeding people
- Giving away things you don't need
- Listening
- And so many other ways

There are many different ways that you can serve others, and you'll want to learn to identify the right type of service for a given situation. No matter what, though, when you are of service, you'll be doing the right thing and you'll be making the world a better place.

DO SOMETHING FOR FREE

One of the best ways that you can train yourself to serve others, and to make the world a better place in general, is to do something for free. This can be anything as long as it is serving other people. You may want to volunteer to help the needy. You may want to pick up a student. You may want to help friends build their résumé and interview for jobs. Whatever it is that you choose, do it for free.

Not everything you do to help others has to be free. You may want to coach others and charge them a fee to do so, and that's okay. The point is that sometimes there will be people who need help and are serious about making change, but can't afford to make these changes. This is where you can step in and give a helping hand. More often than not they'll repay you, whether by buying you dinner or by acknowledging you in their bestselling book.

Remember, you aren't helping others for the glory. This isn't to build some inflated sense of ego or pride. You are doing it because it's the right thing to do, and because it helps to make the world a better place.

My mentor, Mr. Leroy Washington, didn't charge me a dime. He helped me because he saw potential in me. He wasn't poor or starving because of this. He simply chose to give back to the community by helping young people like me get their lives in order and start working toward their dreams.

You can be that for other people. You can be the person that they look back on fondly, thinking about how special you were.

Then, when they are in a position to give, they will know that giving is the right thing to do. They'll help someone else in need, and the world will continue to become a better place. A ripple effect will be set in motion, and it will continue on and on. Your act of kindness will be passed on to the next generation and further. All it takes is a little bit of your time and energy.

When you think about different ways to help others, pick one or more and do them for free. Trust me, you'll get something back that is MUCH MORE valuable than money.

REAL Fulfillment Comes from Giving Value

Whether you are giving back to the community for free, or you are providing a paid product or service, always create REAL value. When you do, you will be more likely to succeed, and you'll feel a true sense of pride.

A lot of people try to skate by and give the bare minimum. They want to put in the least amount of effort necessary, and they want to be praised for a lackluster job. This is a form of entitlement.

Many people feel they deserve what other people have, simply for showing up. What they aren't acknowledging are the extra hours that successful people put in to create the most value possible. They didn't settle for the bare minimum, so when the time comes to reap the rewards, they get more - because they put in more.

Creating value also leads to a deeper sense of fulfillment. You'll know that you did it to the best of your ability, and that will bring a sense of pride. Pride isn't a bad thing; in fact, it's a strong motivator. Only when it gets to cockiness, or the inability to accept failure, you've got too much pride.

A little bit of pride, though, will help you to stay at the top of your game and accomplish great things.

PRIDE AND CREATING VALUE

When you take pride in what you do, the value of the product that you produce naturally goes up. Pride is a strong motivator to be at the top of your game. It's when you start utilizing pride to push you that you'll get better results than you ever thought possible.

Pride can come from a couple of different places. One is the knowledge that you gave back. Simply knowing that you volunteered your time to make the world a better place will give you a boost in pride, which will lead to an overall boost in morale. This will lead you to be more effective in other aspects of your life, because you'll feel that your overall worth is higher.

The other form of pride is that of a job well done. Remember when you were a kid and you got an A+ on a paper? Well, this is the same type of pride, but on a much larger scale.

Your A+ may be cooking the best steaks in town, building the best computers, or being the best coach possible. Whatever field you are in, when you are putting in an A+ effort, you'll feel the same pride that you did when your parents posted your good grades on the refrigerator.

Let this pride motivate you, but don't necessarily let it guide you. Pride can be addictive, and you don't want to start doing things simply to feel good about yourself. Doing good to get a prize isn't the same as doing good because it is the right thing to do. Keep your motives in check, and don't let pride lead you to making bad decisions.

Use your pride as a tool to strive for the best, and take pride in everything that you try to accomplish.

OPEN UP OPPORTUNITIES WITH VALUE

When you create value, the most obvious side effect is that you become valuable. People like producers, and they like success stories. They always want to root for the winner, and they always want to support the people who are on top.

When you are able to create value, people will want to be around you because you are a creator. This allows them to interact with you in new and exciting ways that help to boost them and you.

Let's say that you create the finest shoes around. Your shoes are premium, so you are able to charge a premium price for them. One day an executive from a large corporation that produces shoes sees a pair of your amazing shoes, and she is impressed. She sees the value that you've created, and wants to be involved. She then makes you a big offer, and you begin producing shoes for one of the biggest fashion companies in the world!

Now think about it from another angle. Let's say that you are producing shoes, but you skimp on them. You produce shoes that are just good enough to get by, and you charge a similar price. Do you think you'll find the same opportunity? The answer is NO.

The same goes for creating value in people's lives. When you become a true friend, co-worker, family member, and overall great person to be around, you'll see your opportunities grow. Your friend may call you first when she has a ticket to a big event. Your boss may eye you for a promotion because she knows that you can produce. Really, the possibilities are endless!

Now, you shouldn't produce value simply because it will get you ahead. But producing value will do just that; it will get you ahead. When you are creating the most valuable product on the market, or being the most valuable friend, or the hardest worker, people will want to be involved. They will want to help you, and they will want to work with you to create even more value.

Speaking of doing work ...

NEVER Do the Bare Minimum

Part of taking pride in your work, and part of creating the most value, is NEVER doing only the bare minimum. If all you want to do is skate by, you are either doing the wrong thing, you're being lazy, or you may be afraid to reach your true potential.

Many people are scared to give things their all, because they are scared that their all might not being enough. This fear is irrational. If you never give anything your all, you'll never get the benefits of giving it your all! The worst thing that can happen is that you put in the extra work and then find out that the field you are in isn't really for you.

The best case scenario? You become the best - the leader - in your field!

The greats never settled for second best. From Muhammed Ali to Bill Gates, great men and women push themselves to be greater. Ali said, "I'm the greatest!" and you know what? He meant it. He believed that he was the greatest boxer of all time, and he is now in the history books as one of the greatest and most influential boxers of all time.

Now imagine if Ali did the bare minimum to get by. Imagine he simply put in just enough work to go pro. Do you think you'd remember his name? How many lower rung pro boxers can you name? Unless you're a diehard fan of the sport, probably none.

Whatever you do, do it to the best of your ability. If you are working for a taco joint, make the best tacos anyone has ever tasted! If you are repairing someone's roof, do it better and faster than anyone in your area.

Always go one hundred percent. Always push yourself to be better in any field that you choose. Don't settle for good enough. Never settle. If you want greatness in your life, then you need to perform even the simplest of tasks in a great way. The way you do anything is the way you do everything.

TAKE PRIDE IN YOUR WORK

Everything you do, you should do with care and love. Take pride in your work, and never deliver something that embarrasses you. It's okay to be shy, but if you are truly embarrassed by the product that you produce, it may be time to go back to the drawing board.

I'm not saying you have to be a perfectionist. Perfectionism can be counterproductive. I'm also not saying that you can't learn as you go. You will always be learning, and you will always be growing your greatness.

I AM saying that no matter what your level, do your best and be proud of what you've accomplished. If you paint a picture, paint the best picture that you can and be proud of the final product.

This pride in your work will shine through. Even if you aren't the greatest yet, people will see the effort that you put in, and that may be enough to open up new opportunities for you.

HAPPINESS AND VALUE

In order to be happy in your work, you need to know deep down that you are trying your hardest and creating value. It's important to know that your product or service helps people, and they will want to help you when they see the value that you have created.

Don't EVER settle for "good enough." Always strive to be the greatest.

FIND OPPORTUNITIES TO SERVE

There are many different ways that you can be of service. Some of these will help you make more money. Others will simply make the world a better place, which is at least as important.

Here are some ideas on how you can serve people and institutions to make the world a better place and to create value:

YOUR PARTNER

Whether you are business partners or romantic partners, serving your partner will help to build your relationship and create great things.

Serving your partner can be as easy as being there for them when they need you, doing a little extra to pitch in, and showing them kindness and respect. When you serve your partner, you build the relationship and make the bond stronger. This will lead to success in both your personal life and your professional life.

CUSTOMERS

Customers are always looking for the best value and the best service. Even if you charge a premium price, if you provide outstanding customer service and a superior product, people will be more than willing to spend the extra money.

I'm sure you've experienced companies that have provided bad service or a terrible product. I bet you were reluctant to give them your business again. You may have even given them a bad review or spoken badly about them.

On the other hand, when a business went above and beyond, you probably went out of your way to tell people how great they were.

Always provide your customers with the best service and value possible to get repeat business, great word of mouth, and new business.

FAMILY

As with your partner, you should always be striving to serve your family. This can be as simple as showing up for your son's basketball game or helping your daughter study for her science exam.

Creating value for your family means being a strong role model, and being willing to help whenever they need it. Simply living a better life can make your family better. The other members of your family may look up to you. If they see you doing great things, it will inspire them to greatness as well.

FRIENDS

Just like your family, being a good friend is about showing up. You can listen when your friend needs to vent, put a smile on their face, or just hang out with them.

Different friendships offer different types of value, but the goal overall is to create value in your friend's life. They should want to be around you because you are always there for them, and because you actively encourage them to aspire to greatness.

STUDENTS

One of the best ways that you can be of service is by being a mentor. Whether it is a free or paid mentorship, always be thinking about how you can impart wisdom to your student, and how you can encourage them to reach their goals.

When you are a mentor, you are in a significant position of power which allows you to create great value. Always think about how you can best serve your students, and put yourself in their shoes. You were once where they are. What helped you the most to grow and achieve greatness?

COMMUNITY

When you are serving your community, you should be doing it because you want your community to be a better place. This is where you need to be selfless.

You can serve through youth outreach programs, picking up garbage, serving in political office, or any other form of help. Just make sure you are serving others - not yourself.

You should always be doing at least ONE THING to serve your community for FREE. You'll feel a great sense of pride, and you'll start to genuinely appreciate the beauty and the potential of your community.

CHURCH

If you belong to a church, you should see how you can be of service to the members of your church. You may help by answering phones, or you may simply bring cookies for the bake sale.

Whatever you are able to do, take some time to show appreciation for the rest of the congregation and to celebrate your God by being of service.

THE BEAUTY OF SERVICE

Service is a thing of beauty because it shows your love and respect for the world while helping you create the most value possible. There are always opportunities to serve if you simply seek them out. I guarantee that if you ask around, or search online, you'll find ways to serve your community, your friends, and other people in your life.

Pick up at least one unpaid service position, and always create value. Serve your customers and build your business by giving the best service possible. Never settle for the bare minimum. Share your value and share the wealth by being there for others, and by putting your all into everything that you do.

LAW 12:
LAUGH OUT LOUD AND
ENJOY EVERY MOMENT

A very hearty congratulations to you on making it all this way!

You've learned so much, and you've grown.

I'm proud of you. You may not hear that enough in your life, but I definitely am. I am proud of the person that you are becoming, and the decisions that you are making. Not everyone will take the time to change their lives. Not everyone will take the path you are currently taking.

While realizing your goals is important, as is living your dreams, in this last chapter I want to focus purely on your quality of life.

I want you to be happy. Above everything else, above material success, above achieving what you've set out to do, I want you to be **happy**. Happiness is the real key to a good life. When you are happy, everything else will follow.

Happiness isn't defined but what you do, but rather by who you are and how you choose to feel. I've known plenty of people who are poor and working hard to achieve their goals, but they are happy. I also know people who have practically nothing but are grateful for what they do have.

When I was in Detroit, broke and practically homeless, I felt a freedom that is hard to describe. I was so happy simply to have food in my stomach, clothes on my back, and something to work toward. I try to hold on to that feeling of freedom and gratitude.

It's extremely important to find happiness in the NOW, instead of waiting to accomplish something and then defining your happiness through your success. Even in failure you can be happy because you are doing what you love, and you are living the life that you were meant to live.

I want to discuss living each moment of your life with peace and joy. I also want to discuss the power of laughter, and how laughter can save your life. (I'm not saying this as hyperbole. I truly believe that **laughter can <u>save your life</u>**.)

Then I want to discuss the choice to feel good, in spite of any pain that you are experiencing in your life. Remember, things could always be worse. As long as you're still breathing, there's **HOPE**. This is a word I've repeated throughout this book, because it will help to push you through even the toughest of times.

Sometimes hope is ALL that will get you through a difficult phase. Hope has power beyond measure. Hope has led many to greatness, and hope will hold your hand and guide you through the darkest of times.

So let's get started by discussing one of the most important concepts that should influence everything you do, every single day:

LIFE IS SHORT

Life is the longest thing you'll ever do, but it's still pretty darn short. Think about how long humans have been on the earth. Then think about how old the earth is. Then the universe.

In comparison to all of this, our lives are a tiny little blip in time. We exist for the shortest span of time, yet we can make a great impact. We can change the course of history with our attitude and our actions.

Are you familiar with the butterfly effect? If you went back in time and stepped on just one butterfly, you would change the course of history. Everything is connected, and even the premature death of a butterfly can change events thousands of years down the line.

Now replace that butterfly with a human. Maybe that human is you. Consider all of the choices that you make and all of the people that you affect. You create great change in the fabric of the universe, and your short time here on earth makes a major difference for everything that happens in the future.

Every day, remind yourself how short life is, and take the following list of ideas into consideration. These will change the quality of the life that you live, which will not only change your timeline, but the entirety of the universe around you.

ENJOY EACH MOMENT

You only live in the present.

While you can probably remember much your past, it's always a bit hazy. It's also subjectively based on the feelings you experienced when it was happening. For example, when a crime happens, consider how different people see things differently. Even only a few hours later, the details become fuzzy and they often vary based on the person's own personal memory. Memories are elastic, so they aren't always reliable.

The future is completely uncertain. While you can make plans, nothing is set in stone. You may not be around tomorrow, and the feeling that you are trying to capture isn't a future tense. You choose to feel the way that you feel RIGHT NOW. Not tomorrow, not in an hour, not when you get a raise at work, not when you close that big deal, but RIGHT NOW.

Happiness is a choice. You may have heard this before and thought it was silly. "If happiness is a choice," you might wonder, "why aren't I happy all the time?"

The main reason people don't choose to be happy is because they choose to live outside of the present moment. The present moment is all we have, and we need to enjoy it. We can't wait for some sort of change. That change may never come. Instead, we have to look at things as they are right now and see the beauty in them.

If you are going through a tough time, think about how strong you will become on the other side. Enjoy the things that are going well, and be grateful for what you have. Did you eat today? Are you clothed? Do you have somewhere to sleep?

Some people will tell you that these things are too basic to create happiness. They'll question why you should be happy over such trivial things. Well, to a lot of people throughout history, these things weren't trivial. Going back even a few hundred years, a lot of people went to bed hungry. Some were forced to wear dirty, old clothes and seek shelter from the elements.

Today there are many places in the world where children are starving, people are huddled together for warmth, and life from day to day is uncertain and even dangerous. If you are born in a place that has allowed you access to this book, congratulations! You've won the cosmic lottery!

This is especially true for western countries. You've got access to free education, and you have more opportunity than any other person at any other point in history.

You are living the dream right now and you can't see the forest for the trees!

Enjoy the gifts that you've been given, and enjoy this moment, right now. Be grateful, be humble, and be aware. Most of all, be happy.

DON'T WASTE YOUR TIME

Your time is a valuable resource, and this resource is very limited. I'm going to talk about wasting time at work in a moment, but for right now, I want to remind you not to waste your time overall.

Don't get caught up in the he-said, she-said. Don't get caught up in the drama. Don't take away the moments that you are given.

<u>Time is the most valuable resource you are given</u>.

One more time, for good measure:

Time is the most valuable resource you are given.

It's more important than money. It's more important than gold. Time is the only thing that you will always want more of, but you'll never have. Your expiration date is already set, and there's nothing that you can do to avoid it. Because of this, you need to spend this resource wisely.

What if I told you that you only have $100,000 for the rest of your life? How would you spend it, knowing that you'd never have another dime coming in? Time is the same way. You only have so many years, so many months, so many weeks, days, hours, minutes, seconds. That's all you get.

Spend it wisely.

REALLY Take Things In

There is so much beauty all around you, at all times. At any given second, there is something beautiful going on around you.

Look around. Is the sun shining? Awesome. Is it raining? The sound of rain is amazing. Rain waters the plants and makes the grass green. Are there flowers? Other people? Dogs? Babies? All of these things are beautiful too.

Everything around you has an element of beauty to it. Soak it in.

When you listen to music, get lost in it. Allow the emotions to flood over you. Listen to each instrument and take in the talent, work, passion, and beauty. Take in photos, film, and quality television. Enjoy the feelings and appreciate the work that people put into creating something - even if it's not necessarily to your liking.

You don't have to love everything, but learn to appreciate it. It's all there for a reason. Just like you're here for a reason. Be present and enjoy the moment. Enjoy the walk you are taking, or enjoy the comfort of your couch. (Not for too long, though. You have things to do!)

There is always something great going on around you. Focus on that beauty and greatness and appreciate it for what it is.

CREATE MEMORIES

I know I just spent a lot of time telling you to live in the present, but sometimes it is nice to reflect.

There are so many exciting moments that you've had in your life, and it's great to take a little time here and there and reflect on them. When you do, reflect on the good times. Cherish those times. Cherish the times with loved ones, and the times you did great things.

Moving forward, create great memories. Create the kind of memories that you can tell your grandkids one day. You can do this by living the kind of life that creates great stories.

Living in the present and living a life of greatness also creates amazing memories. Even if you forget a few, you'll have enough to leave you feeling satisfied when it's time to leave this earth.

I have some amazing memories from my life: From all the times I had with my mother Mamie Brown, to the rush of being on the radio for the first time, to watching my children grow into amazing, beautiful adults. These are all memories that I will cherish until my last breath.

Memories will remind you of the greatness that you have accomplished. They will fill you with joy, and they will give you hope. Most of all, they'll stand as a testament to the kind of life that you chose to live.

DON'T MAKE LIFE A SLOG

If you feel like life's a drag, then this section is for you. Just like choosing to be happy, you have the choice to make your life a slog, or to make it fun.

If you don't know what a slog is, it's when you do something even though you find it difficult and boring. Does this reflect the kind of life that you live? Do you find that most of the activities that you do are either boring, difficult, or both? If so, it's time to make a change.

A lot of people will tell you that this is just how life is. Life is tough. Life is about doing what you don't want to do. Life is about just getting by until you die. These people are choosing to be miserable, and you don't have to make the same choice! Instead, you can choose to celebrate life.

You can choose greatness, and you can choose excitement. Sure, there will be times that you have to do boring or difficult things, but you don't have to center your life around those times or those things.

Let's talk about this a little further, starting with your work.

DON'T WORK JOBS YOU HATE

I know that there are times that you do what you have to do to get by, but you shouldn't be allowing these times to get in the way of your dreams.

If you are working a job you hate just to get by, then you better be planning something greater. You've read most of this book for a reason, so you now have many of the tools you need. Start actively looking for a new job, going to school, starting to create your own job, or a mixture of these.

No matter how trapped you feel, remember that in reality, you aren't. There is always a way out.

You may feel comfortable in your job. You may have been doing it for years. This doesn't make it right for you, though. Just because you do something over and over doesn't mean that it'll make you content.

Unless something changes dramatically, you won't magically wake up one day and think, "Hey! This job that I've hated for the last few years isn't so bad!"

Most jobs are around 40 hours of work per week. Multiply that by the 52 weeks in a year. Now, let's say you have another 30 years until you retire. That adds up to 62,400 hours. Divide that by 24 hours and you've got 2600 days. Divide that by 365 and that's over SEVEN YEARS, solid, of working a job that you hate.

That's crazy! Imagine what you could do with those seven years. Think about being on your deathbed, minutes before you expire. Suddenly, the doctor walks in and says, "Oops, sorry, we read the charts wrong! You actually have seven MORE years to live."

That's a lot of time!

There's nothing wrong with seven years' worth of work if you love doing it. If you are working toward accomplishing your goals, and you are living a life happier than your wildest dreams, seven years will fly by! But if you are stuck in a job you hate, those seven years will feel like an eternity.

Don't waste your time in a job only to make money to get by. Find a job or an income stream that you are passionate about, and enjoy the time that you spend at it.

THE "LIFE IS TOUGH" FALLACY

I'm sure you've heard the expression "life is tough and then you die." This is a fallacy by which many people actually live their lives. If you have scoffed and said it jokingly, ask yourself if somewhere deep down you actually meant it.

Maybe you'd just gone through a recent series of heartaches that clouded your vision and allowed the negativity to creep in. Whatever the case may be, the "Life is Tough" line is WRONG.

If you believe that life is nothing but unenjoyable work, heartache, and death, you're doing it wrong!

Don't get me wrong. I know that there will be times your life is difficult or challenging. Everyone has those times.

There will be times that you'll face a crossroads with what seem like insurmountable odds. This doesn't make your life any less worth living. In fact, it should serve as a reminder that you're alive. You only feel pain because you are on this plane of existence. It's part of the experience. Sure, your whole life shouldn't be comprised of suffering, but pain is inevitable.

I once heard a discussion on the difference between pain and suffering, and I loved it so much that I want to share it with you. I was told that pain is the hardship we go through. We all experience pain. It's part of being human.

Suffering, on the other hand, is when you choose to hold on to the pain. It's when you dwell, when you ruminate, and when you let that pain fester. After a while, the pain intensifies and becomes its own entity known as suffering.

Remember:

Pain is inevitable; SUFFERING is a CHOICE.

When you learn to distinguish between the two, and you begin to see how much of your hurt is pain and how much is suffering, you'll be able to alleviate the suffering. You'll be able to accept the pain, and in doing so, the suffering will diminish. Pain will pass. Suffering won't, unless you choose to let it go.

Your life doesn't have to be a pileup of hardships that lead to your inevitable demise. Instead, it should be something that you enjoy that occasionally provides challenges in the form of pain. If you can see these challenges for what they are, you can work through the pain and avoid suffering altogether.

LOVE WHAT YOU DO

We've discussed this a lot already, but I want to remind you to love what you do. Enjoy the process and stick to doing what you love. Sure, times will come up that you have to do things that you don't want to do. That's part of life, but it isn't all of life.

Life presents us with thousands, even millions, of choices to take the path of happiness. We are presented with so many opportunities to do what we love that it's unreal! But some of us don't.

Some of us choose a harder path, and some of us choose to suffer. Don't do this to yourself. Don't become a martyr for a cause that doesn't even exist.

Choose love. Choose doing what you love to do, and choose loving others. Choose the positive that will enhance, not diminish, your life. Love the process, and don't go down the routes that lead to suffering.

You are in control, as much as you don't believe it. Don't make life into a slog. Make it into a celebration and have fun!

LAUGH OUT LOUD

Speaking of celebration and having fun, I want to discuss something that we all do, but some of us don't do enough: Laugh.

You've probably heard the quote, "Laughter is the best medicine." You might be surprised to discover how true this really is. A positive attitude and the ability to laugh will elevate your mood, and this elevation in mood can help you in a myriad of ways. This includes everything from combating depression to even helping you get through illness and pain.

You see, when we are in a compromised state, our body looks to our mood to tell us how to respond. If you are melancholy and you've given up hope, your body will follow suit. If, on the other hand, you are jovial and optimistic, you send a signal to your body that the show isn't over; you still have more life to live.

Laughter can actually help heal you on a cellular level, and can increase your ability to handle physical and emotional pain. It can literally help to heal you, and help you through the toughest of times. You may have an injury, illness, or sadness that is weighing you down. Laughter will help you to cope and to feel better, even in the most difficult times.

Do you have a friend who is always able to make you smile, no matter how tough things get? Maybe a close loved one died, and you fell into a deep despair. Then your friend called and before you knew it, you were laughing through the tears. Suddenly, even if only briefly, everything felt like it was going to be okay.

These interactions are invaluable, and this helps to further show the power of positivity and laughter. Even when things are grim, those who are able to keep a smile on their faces will push through to the other side.

Comedians don't make jokes because they are oblivious to the cruelty of the world; they make jokes in spite of the darkness. They are able to tap into something much deeper and much greater.

The best comedians are able to look at how ridiculous the world can be, and help us laugh instead of cry. They can take something that could be heartbreaking, and they can help us to see the light in it. This isn't because they don't see the negative.

It's because they see the negative - and choose to turn it into a positive.

SOMETIMES ALL YOU CAN DO IS LAUGH

There will be times in your life that literally all you can do is laugh. Any other response will only make the situation worse. It's extremely difficult to train yourself to laugh at these times, but it's necessary.

I want to share with you something that a great philosopher named Alan Watts once said. I'm going to paraphrase, so this isn't an exact quote, but you'll get the idea.

Alan Watts discussed the choice of how to respond to a loved one on their deathbed. He discussed how when it's time to go, it shouldn't be a sad occasion. This is especially true if you are religious or believe in some sort of reincarnation.

Instead of focusing on the sadness of death, there should be a great celebration of life. The family members of the afflicted should gather and have a going away party. Drinks, music, laughter ... think about the best birthday party ever, except it's celebrating the closing of the book, instead of the first chapter.

We all feel sadness when we finish our favorite book, but we still take a moment to savor its greatness. Alan Watts discusses the choice of making someone's final moments beautiful, and allowing the final thing that they see to be your smiling faces instead of your tears.

This is a beautiful sentiment, and it really illustrates my point. The absolute saddest thing that you can go through, the death of a loved one, doesn't have to be a sad occasion. The paradigm can shift. Instead of being a gathering of the sadness of death, you can instead turn it into a celebration of life.

Sometimes all you can do is laugh. Life can be ridiculous, it can be unfair, and it can be challenging. There is always humor in it, though. There is always positivity somewhere, and when things get tough, you'll need to tap into that positivity. It will change the way you view a situation, and it will help you to push through even the most difficult times.

INTERRUPT YOUR WORRIES

There will always be worries that plague you. There will be unpaid bills, sickness, uncertainty, loss. Everything negative that can imaginably happen will likely happen to some extent during your life. You can't avoid this. It is going to happen with or without your consent.

What you CAN choose is how you react to these situations. You have the power to take a negative and either neutralize it or turn it into a positive.

You can do this by throwing yourself into the moment, living a life of joy, and utilizing the power of laughter.

You ultimately choose the quality of life that you want to live. I know at times it may seem like things are out of control, and you can't always control the circumstances. But you CAN control **HOW YOU REACT TO THEM**. It's within your power to make this choice. YOU decide what you do with what you are given.

And you MUST choose joy.

You MUST choose love.

You MUST choose **happiness**.

Life Is Made Up of Choices

Basically, your life comes down to a series of choices. Sure, you won't always make the right decisions, but if you follow your heart and you make decisions out of love, you'll find that you land on the right path.

God (or whatever power you believe in) has a plan for you. God wants you to be happy, and God wants you to play the role in the universe that you were born to play. You may want to rebel. You may want to throw a tantrum and sit on your laurels. You may want to look up at the sky and ask, "Why? Why is life so difficult? It's not fair!"

When you really take a look at your life, though, you'll see that God isn't to blame. He gives you opportunity after opportunity to make the changes that you need to make. It's up to YOU to recognize them and to make them.

I want to tell you one of my favorite jokes. There's a lesson in it, if you pay attention:

A man is on the roof of his house, and there is water all around the house. A massive storm hit his area, and it caused flooding that can only be described as "biblical." Still, he stayed calm. He was a man of faith, and he knew that God would save him.

The water was approaching the top windows of his two story house when a raft came by. It wasn't much: Plastic, small, and yellow with just barely enough room for two.

The man on the raft called to the man on the roof and said, "I have room on my raft. Do you need help?"

The man on the roof replied, "No thank you, God will save me."

The man on the raft shrugged and paddled on.

The water was up to the storm gutters when a boat came by. There were a few passengers on the boat wrapped in blankets, and the captain called out to the man on the roof. "Quick, jump on! We have room for one more!"

"No," the man on the roof replied, "God will save me."

Befuddled, the captain of the boat shrugged and steered away from the house.

The water rose further and began to lick the bottom of the man's feet. He started becoming discouraged. Where was God? Suddenly, a light appeared in the sky.

"Finally!" he thought. Then he saw that the light was a helicopter. A rope ladder was being lowered to him, but he politely declined it.

"No," he said, "God will save me."

The helicopter hovered for a moment but eventually left to save other people.

To no one's surprise, the man on the roof drowned.

He was surrounded by light. Everything around him had a beautiful glow, and he knew immediately where he was. He was in heaven. Still, this wasn't enough for him. The man from the roof wanted answers! He demanded to speak with God, and when he got an audience with God, he went on a tirade.

"Why would you let me drown, God? I prayed to you! I believed in you! I thought you would save me and you abandoned me. Why, God? Why?"

God sighed, and then replied, "I sent you a raft, a boat, and a helicopter. What more did you want?"

The point of this joke is pretty obvious, but if you didn't catch it, it's that God helps those that help themselves.

You will be presented with opportunities to change your life. You will have the opportunity to leave the house being swallowed up by the flood, but you have to jump on the raft, boat, or helicopter! Where you are now may depend on how high the water is, but you haven't drowned yet.

There is an opportunity waiting for you, but you HAVE to take it.

Your life will come down to a few key choices and your response to them. This will determine the trajectory of where things go. This doesn't mean that you can't change your path. It's never too late. Still, the water will continue to rise and YOU have to save yourself.

This book gave you the tools to do this. You learned how to listen to your heart, overcome your fears, develop your team, get rid of toxins, light up the room, and enjoy the process. You also learned how to smile, and how to live a better life. You've learned all of these things, and now it's up to YOU to choose this path.

It's up to YOU to live the life that God intended you to live.

While you are alive, there is still time. You can still make the right choices, but you have to listen to what the universe is telling you. You need to be **BRAVE** and you must have **HOPE**.

With bravery, hope, and the tools I have given you, you CANNOT fail. This is Mamie Brown's boy telling you that it's YOUR life.

GO OUT THERE AND LIVE IT!